Dialogue Mapping

'In this book, Dr Conklin clearly dimensionalizes the critical dynamics at play as we face our most difficult business issues . . . our so called "wicked problems". He then outlines an insightful and detailed prescriptive path forward called dialogue mapping that leaders can apply to wicked problems throughout their organizations. I think this is an excellent guide for all those interested in durable collaborative solutions in our increasingly tough business climates today.'

*John C. Mitchell, former President, Business
Printer Division, Lexmark International, Inc.*

'My focus has long been on augmenting humanity's Collective IQ, feeling strongly that if human society can't significantly improve its collective capability for understanding and coping with its most complex, urgent problems then our worldwide society will likely crash. I met Jeff some twenty years ago, and resonated instantly. What he has in this book is of powerfully basic importance to improving our Collective IQ – and thus, in my view, to helping significantly change our world to be a better place for us humans.'

*Douglas Engelbart, PhD, Director of Bootstrap Institute,
inventor of the computer mouse and the first hypertext system,
winner of the Turing Award and the National Medal of Technology*

'Project teams, boards of directors, consultants and many other professionals deal with "wicked problems" that revolve around making meaning. There isn't a "right" answer. Finding a solution means finding a sensible way forward. Intelligent solutions come through conversations: by engaging, questioning, deliberating, debating, discussing, and deciding. Dialogue mapping is an invaluable tool for groups of people finding their way through wicked problems. Jeff Conklin pioneered this field, showing the connection between conversations (dialogue) and solving wicked problems. I learned a lot from him and I'm delighted to see his work in book form. The ideas are intellectually rewarding and, just as important, are tried and tested. Dialogue mapping is a practical, participative approach for dealing with wicked problems.'

*Mark Addleson, PhD, Director, Organizational Learning
Program, George Mason University, School of Public Policy*

'Dialogue mapping was the essential ingredient that held together the NASA-funded government/industry partnership that will allow unmanned aircraft to have safe access into the United States national airspace system for the benefit of all mankind.'

John Walker, Policy Team Leader, Access 5

'Over the past ten years I have been bringing dialogue mapping to some of the most senior conversations on the planet. From the future of corn to better forms of government, dialogue mapping helps large and disparate groups of people agree on the problem, develop and implement a solution, and get results quickly. It is an amazing methodology explained brilliantly by Jeff Conklin.'

Christopher McGoff, CEO, Touchstone Consulting

'In the public policy field in which I work, "wicked problems" are a way of life. Seemingly endless meetings, floating membership in stakeholder groups, hidden agendas (even from people who think they have agendas), repetition without much visible progress, and "satisficing" solutions that result when the effort runs of out of time or energy or other resources. Jeff Conklin's *Dialogue Mapping: Building Shared Understanding of Wicked Problems* is a godsend. It provides not only an understanding of why working through wicked problems is so difficult, but the tools to allow people of incredible diversity to reach shared commitments to results through the building of shared understanding. I've used dialogue mapping for nearly 20 years. I highly recommend investing in this incredibly valuable tool. You won't be disappointed.'

Michael M. Hertel, PhD, Director,
Corporate Environmental Policy, SCE

About the Author

Dr Jeff Conklin is a lifelong student of organizational communication and collaboration, and the tools that support them. Through the work of the CogNexus Institute, he remains active as a practitioner of dialogue mapping, although his passion is teaching dialogue mapping as the art and science of creating shared understanding.

Dialogue Mapping

Building Shared Understanding of Wicked Problems

Jeff Conklin

John Wiley & Sons, Ltd

Copyright © 2006   John Wiley & Sons Ltd, The Atrium, Southern Gate, Chichester, West Sussex PO19 8SQ, England

Telephone: (+44) 1243 779777

Email (for orders and customer service enquiries): cs-books@wiley.co.uk

Visit our Home Page on www.wiley.com

Other Wiley Editorial Offices

John Wiley & Sons Inc., 111 River Street, Hoboken, NJ 07030, USA

Jossey-Bass, 989 Market Street, San Francisco, CA 94103-1741, USA

Wiley-VCH Verlag GmbH, Boschstr. 12, D-69469 Weinheim, Germany

John Wiley & Sons Australia Ltd, 42 McDougall Street, Milton, Queensland 4064, Australia

John Wiley & Sons (Asia) Pte Ltd, 2 Clementi Loop #02-01, Jin Xing Distripark, Singapore 129809

John Wiley & Sons Canada Ltd, 22 Worcester Road, Etobicoke, Ontario, Canada M9W 1L1

Wiley also publishes its books in a variety of electronic formats. Some content that appears in print may not be available in electronic books

Library of Congress Cataloging-in-Publication Data

Conklin, E. Jeffrey.
    Dialogue mapping : building shared understanding of wicked problems / Jeffrey Conklin.
      p. cm.
    Includes bibliographical references and index.
    ISBN-13: 978-0-470-01768-5 (pbk. : alk. paper)
    ISBN-10: 0-470-01768-6 (pbk. : alk. paper)
    1. Business meetings. 2. Project management. I. Title.
HF5734.5.C66 2006
658.4'5 – dc22

2005013962

British Library Cataloguing in Publication Data

A catalogue record for this book is available from the British Library

ISBN-13 978-0-470-01768-5
ISBN-10 0-470-01768-6

Typeset in 11/16pt Kuenstler by SNP Best-set Typesetter Ltd., Hong Kong

Dedicated to my teachers, Joanne and Eli

Contents

Preface

Two decades ago, when I started working in the field of software design, the implicit assumption was that problems were stable and well defined and most of the work in a big project was in coming up with the solution. In addition, the process of working out the solution to a complex problem was understood to be fundamentally linear – a sequence of steps, which, if followed competently, would result in a successful outcome.

But there is increasing awareness that a shared understanding of the problem cannot be taken for granted. Too many large projects – fully equipped with the best engineering and project management minds – have foundered on the hidden shoals of *social complexity*. It turns out that the absence of shared understanding and buy-in about the problem definition, scope, and goals can kill a project just as surely as poor technology or faulty implementation.

Organizations are now beginning to embrace the idea that these two aspects of projects – problem understanding and solution formulation – are not distinct phases, but rather different kinds of conversation that must be woven together from beginning to end. Problem structuring is a critical aspect of the design process that takes into account the diversity of goals, assumptions, and meanings among stakeholders. At the heart of this new understanding of organizational life is the recognition that project work is fundamentally social, and that communication among stakeholders must be managed and nurtured in order for the social network to cohere into a functioning entity.

Moreover, experimental evidence suggests that our reliance on the linear approach to project management – gather the data, analyze the data, formulate a solution, implement the solution – is unfounded. Our modern problems, both social and technological, are 'wicked' . . . you don't understand the problem until you have come up with a possible solution. So much for a linear sequence of stages from problem definition to final solution! Instead the process is inevitably 'opportunity driven', requiring a new set of skills and tools to make sense of the chaos.

This book is about meetings, which is where the social network does its sense making. Without laboring the point, it would be fair to say that meetings don't work very well in general, especially if the problem is complex and the stakes are high. Sometimes there is an invisible battleground in which combatants, under cover of specialized knowledge and social alliances, seek to take new territory or defend what they have. The dimensions of the battlefield may be unclear to the participants, but there is no mistaking that we are *not* all on the same team, and there *will* be winners and losers. This feudal approach to sorting out problems may have been adequate in the past, but it doesn't come close to creating the clarity and commitment necessary to pull off the postmodern project. It is time that we – as managers, leaders, and, indeed, as a species – get much better at managing the social complexity that comes with modern projects, including setting up meetings to be as collaborative as possible.

Effective communication is not easy, but neither is it the exclusive art of gifted facilitators. The central thesis of this book is that what is missing from our social network toolkit is an environment or 'container' in which stakeholders can step back to see the Big Picture, the larger context in which they are all on the same team and they all want the same or similar outcomes. (It is not about consensus. Sometimes we have to start with agreeing to disagree. But then we must roll up our sleeves and identify precisely what we disagree about and why.)

Dialogue mapping is about creating this larger picture. It is an interaction technique that can break the illusion that stakeholders are isolated and opposed. Dialogue mapping orients a group more to a same-side spirit of learning together, of mapping the intense complexity of a project instead of succumbing to it, of creating shared understanding about what the problem is, and crafting a shared commitment to a solution. Dialogue mapping provides the raw materials of group memory, so the group doesn't keep reinventing the wheel, and the participants can really listen to each other, instead of each scrambling to defend his or her bit of territory. Dialogue mapping gives a project team a container large enough and rich enough to hold the multithreaded conversations that need to take place, and to support the team in the lurching process of making sense of its world and creating a context of community and support.

The approach described here is not revolutionary – it is an organic part of an emerging body of thought and practice about communication, collaboration, and organizational life. Readers familiar with dynamic facilitation (Rough, 1991, 1997), cognitive mapping (Eden and Ackerman, 1998), or any of the emerging family of problem structuring methods (Rosenhead and Mingers, 2001) will find much that is familiar here. Readers coming from computer science or human computer interface backgrounds may be familiar with the research on design rationale (summarized in Moran and Carroll, 1996), to which dialogue mapping traces its early roots. Dialogue mapping also draws on the field of argumentation, the scholarly approach to reasoning, natural inference and persuasion, and is closely related to a variety of argumentation tools (Kirschner, Buckingham Shum and Carr, 2003). Dialogue mapping practitioners have used it in conjunction with other facilitation and analytic approaches, including scenario planning (Schwartz, 1996; van der Heijden, 1996), appreciative inquiry (Cooperrider and Whitney, 1999), future search conferences (Weisbord and Janoff, 2000), analytic hierarchy process (Saaty, 1999), and process improvement. Readers familiar with the field of sense making (Weick, 1995; Dervin, 1998) will recognize dialogue mapping as essentially a practical tool for team sense making.

Here's the recipe for dialogue mapping: you combine equal measures of *shared display, argumentation scheme,* and *active listening.* The shared display is familiar equipment in the modern organization – just project a computer screen on the wall in front of the group. The argumentation scheme is probably less familiar: it is a notation for diagramming the structure of a line of reasoning. The word 'argument' comes from the Latin *arguere,* which means to make clear. The particular scheme used in dialogue mapping is issue-based information system (IBIS), and it consists of questions and answers and pros and cons – commonplace discussion elements. The argumentation scheme serves to unpack the dense and tangled logic of the group interaction. The third component, active listening, is the skill component of the approach – it is a particular style of active listening that engages the meeting participants in the collaborative process of building a diagram (a 'map') of their conversation. These ingredients combine to create an environment that supports the hard work of collective reflection on a complex problem.

How Dialogue Mapping was Discovered

The intention of this book is to equip the reader with the basic skills and distinctions needed to start practicing this art form. The core idea is quite simple – a group uses dialogue mapping to construct a map of the issues related to a project or problem. A dialogue mapping session looks a bit like a group assembling a jigsaw puzzle together: the emerging puzzle is displayed on a computer screen or whiteboard, there's a dialogue mapper capturing the group members' suggestions, and the puzzle pieces themselves are whatever issues or ideas the group members have in the conversation. The dialogue mapper is both designated listener and puzzle master.

The development of dialogue mapping was somewhat accidental. In 1991 I was the Chief Scientist and a founder of Corporate Memory Systems, Inc. Our product, a hypertext groupware system called 'QuestMap', was designed to allow individuals sitting at their computers to hold 'virtual meetings' in which each person's comments were entered into a shared map according to the IBIS argumentation scheme (i.e. questions, ideas, pros and cons). Our company had sold our first and largest installation of our new groupware system to the Environmental Affairs (EA) division at Southern California Edison. Dr Michael Hertel, the Director, was drawn to the additional rigor of having his staff use the IBIS logic to analyze issues and make policy decisions, as well as to the idea of creating organizational memory for EA.

However, the groupware rollout of QuestMap in itself was only a moderate success. Despite training in the IBIS method and the QuestMap tool, many of the EA staff resisted doing their work in a graphical hypertext groupware tool. (Small wonder, given that even Lotus Notes™, with vastly greater financial resources for marketing and education, was at that time struggling to get traction in the just-emerging groupware marketplace. And Notes did not require users to embrace and skillfully practice the art of argumentation.)

One day in 1992 Hertel called me to report a new success in the adoption of QuestMap. He had hooked his computer to a display projector and used the tool with his staff to capture group comments during a meeting. After listening to Hertel's excited description of his discovery of a new way – finally! – to engage his staff with the software, I recall patiently explaining to him that our system was designed and intended for use as an *asynchronous* collaborative tool. (Collaborative technologies come in two flavors: *asynchronous* tools, like email and Lotus Notes™, and *synchronous* tools, like video conferencing and instant messaging. The attraction of asynchronous tools is that participants collaborate on their own schedule, not the group's.) We frequently gave sales demonstrations of the software using display projectors, but as a company we knew – and certainly, as the Chief Scientist, I was convinced – that face-to-face meetings were a very different kind of collaboration for which our software was simply not designed.

Nonetheless, Hertel persisted in using the software both synchronously and asynchronously, and eventually I saw the wisdom of his approach. Unlike the asynchronous mode, the meeting participants did not need to go through several days of training in order to engage in IBIS-based discussions. Since one person was creating the map many of the problems of working in a 'shared information space,' such as shared conventions and etiquette, were avoided. The meeting was improved by having a shared visual focus for the group. Precise meeting minutes that succinctly summarized all the issues were produced as a natural byproduct. (Deeper analysis of this experience can be found in Conklin, 2003.)

Both the software and the techniques for using it in meetings have grown up since 1992, but the basic concept has not changed. Along the way, we have learned that mapping a meeting conversation in IBIS does not require all the groupware capabilities sported by the software, and indeed for short meetings a whiteboard or wall of flipchart paper is perfectly adequate for the approach to work. Since 1995 I have focused my energies on two things: developing and practicing the technique now known as dialogue mapping, and – more challengingly – learning to teach it to others. This pursuit has become my life's passion.

How the Book Unfolds

There are three parts. Part I provides a foundational framework about the problems dialogue mapping is addressing and how it addresses them. Part II is a tutorial on the basic mechanics of dialogue mapping. Part III explores advanced issues of applying the technique in practical settings.

Part I

Chapter 1, 'Wicked Problems and Social Complexity', tells the story of three forces that fragment projects just as surely as rain creates mud: wicked problems, social complexity, and technical complexity. This chapter seeks to illuminate the chronic low-level organizational pain that these forces create. Chapter 2, 'Building Shared Understanding', completes the story by demonstrating that a shared display driven by a skilled operator is a powerful anti-fragmentation force, creating shared understanding about the problem domain and shared commitment to possible solutions. As a balance to this foundational discussion, Chapter 3, 'The Dialogue Mapping Experience', tells the story of a fictional dialogue mapping session.

Part II

Chapter 4, 'IBIS: A Tool for all Reasons', presents a tutorial on the issue-based information system (IBIS) notation of questions and ideas, pros and cons. The next chapter, 'The Dialogue Mapping Listening Cycle', describes the listen–guess–capture–validate listening cycle that a dialogue mapper uses to create an effective shared display with a group, and contains a section entitled 'Transcriptive and Interpretive Capture', which explains when to capture precisely what is being said and when to be interpretive.

Part III

We now roll up our sleeves for some advanced topics. Chapter 6, 'Question Types', shows the recurring pattern of questions common to all creative meetings, and the seven types of question that tie dialogue maps together into a coherent Big Picture. There are three common pitfalls of group collaboration, three troublesome modes of discourse, and Chapter 7, 'Three Moves of Discourse', shows how a skilled dialogue mapper deals with them. 'Limits of Dialogue

Mapping', Chapter 8, talks about when to stop mapping. The final chapter, 'Decisions, Decisions', explores decisions and the process for making decisions using dialogue mapping.

Readers who are impatient with theory and just want to jump into dialogue mapping should go directly to Chapters 3 and 4. That will be enough to get started. Later you can fill in the gaps and explore the more advanced topics. You'll probably also want to download and install Compendium (it's free) – see the Appendix.

Who is this Book For?

This book is for you if you are a consultant, facilitator, team leader, manager, or executive, working in or for an organization of any size, commercial or government.

There are three levels of learning you can take from this book. At the first level, you learn about the issue-based structure of design and problem-solving conversations, and simply from knowing this argumentation scheme you start to listen differently to these kinds of conversations (which are all around us, and often are quite complex), and you may even start to hear and 'see' clear patterns where most people are simply hearing noise and confusion.

At the second level, you learn how this issue-based thinking plays out when it is used in a shared display to facilitate meetings. At this level you can understand and appreciate how this can augment the collective intelligence of a group wrestling with a complex problem. And you'll start to become more sensitized to the times when groups *aren't* collaborating very well.

At the third and deepest level, you practice dialogue mapping with your family or friends or colleagues, and because you are actually doing it you shift from *knowing about* it to being *skillful* at it. As with any craft skill (or language or musical instrument) the more you practice the more skillful you become. Because dialogue mapping is interactive, you have to actually *do* it to have the knowledge move from your brain into the rest of your body.

If you spend any time in meetings with other people, whether it's a multimillion dollar project or a school district planning group, then any of these three levels of learning will benefit you. At the third level, it will also benefit the groups you work with or participate with.

You don't have to decide which level you want now. Read the book, and see if just knowing about the issue-based structure doesn't change the way you listen and interact in meetings. If it helps you listen and understand more deeply, you can experiment with using it on a problem with a friend or colleague. If that helps you come up with a better solution faster, then you will probably be drawn to trying it out with the groups you are involved with as a way to help everyone listen better and collaborate more effectively with each other. I've been practicing this technique since 1993 and I am still learning and getting more skillful.

As human beings we stand at a critical juncture in our evolution. The problems that we have created at our current levels of thinking and technology are more complex than ever before (see Rischard, 2002 for a good formulation of the challenges). Moreover, the consequences of failing to address these problems will be catastrophic, and the solutions leading us toward peace and sustainable happiness will require every bit of collective intelligence and collaborative skill that we can muster. Each of us is called to find our own unique offering in this exciting and dreadful time – our piece of the Great Puzzle. You needn't have 'group facilitator' on your business card to find ways to help. I invite you to absorb the inkling of wisdom in this book, make it your own, and give it away.

Acknowledgements

I am deeply indebted to Lansing Bicknell for his partnership and inspiration in the creation of the original version of the workshop, *Creating Collaborative Meetings*, on which this book is based. Bill Weil's wit still shines through in sections of chapters 1 and 4 that he drafted over a decade ago. Michael Begeman and Marie Case were extraordinary partners in our vision for corporate memory. Touchstone, Inc. has been a potent incubator for the ideas and experiences presented in this book, and I owe special thanks to Chris McGoff and Steve Lynott for their patience and support over the years. I also thank Kim Salins, whose inspiration and friendship has added much to the art of dialogue mapping, and who has contributed much to this book. I am immensely grateful to Al Selvin and Simon Buckingham Shum for their encouragement and their contributions to my thinking about this art form. I thank Rosa Zubizarreta, Bill Pardee, Eugene Eric Kim, and Jack Park for providing thoughtful reviews of the manuscript. Mark Westcombe was instrumental in the publishing process. My wife Joanne helped in so many ways, including unflagging encouragement to get this project finished. All of my work on dialogue mapping follows in the visionary footsteps of Horst Rittel, to whom I owe my career. And to my teacher, Eli Jaxon-Bear, I give my eternal gratitude, for showing the way.

Part I

1
Wicked Problems and Social Complexity

*S*ome *problems are so complex that you have to be highly*
intelligent and well informed just to be undecided about
them.

Laurence J. Peter (*Peter's Almanac*,
entry for 24 September 1982)

This book is about building collective intelligence: the creativity and resourcefulness that a group or team can bring to a complex and novel problem. Collective intelligence is a natural property of socially shared cognition, a natural enabler of collaboration. But there are also natural forces that challenge collective intelligence, forces that doom projects and make collaboration difficult or impossible. These are *forces of fragmentation*.

The concept of fragmentation provides a name and an image for a phenomenon that pulls apart something which is whole. Fragmentation suggests a condition in which the people involved see themselves as more separate than united, and in which information and knowledge are chaotic and scattered. The fragmented pieces are, in essence, the perspectives, understandings, and intentions of the collaborators. Fragmentation, for example, is when the stakeholders in a project are all convinced that their version of the problem is correct.

Fragmentation can be hidden, as when stakeholders don't even realize that there are incompatible tacit assumptions about the problem, and each believes that his or her understandings are complete and shared by all.

The antidote to fragmentation is shared understanding and shared commitment. This book is about a new way to create shared understanding, and this chapter sets the stage by exploring specific ways that the forces of fragmentation work in organizations and projects.

Fragmentation=
Wickedness x Social
Complexity

Fragmentation and Organizational Pain

There is a subtle but pervasive kind of pain in our organizations. It is characterized by such frequently heard complaints as 'How am I supposed to get my work done with all of these meetings?' and 'We always have time to do it over again, but never time to do it right.'

It is a sense of futility of expecting things to be one way and repeatedly banging into a different reality. It is the dull ache of déjà vu when you are handed an impossible deadline or a vague assignment. It is the frustration of calling a meeting to make a decision and watching the meeting unravel into a battle between rival departments, or get lost in a thicket of confusion over the meaning of a technical term. It is the frustration of finally achieving a hard-won decision and then having it fall apart or get 'pocket vetoed' because there wasn't really buy-in. It is the pain of fragmentation.

I was working late one evening when the janitor came in to vacuum the office. I noticed that he was going back and forth over the same areas without appearing to get the lint up off the carpet. I smiled and shouted to him (the vacuum cleaner was a loud one), 'It must be frustrating to have to use that vacuum cleaner.' He looked at me with a sad smile and said 'Not as frustrating as being told to go back and do it over!' It is *that* kind of pain, and it goes all the way up to the executive suite.

Part of the pain is a misunderstanding of the nature of the problems at hand. More precisely, the pain is caused by working on a special class of problems – *wicked problems* – with thinking, tools, and methods that are useful only for simpler ('tame') problems. Problem wickedness is a force of fragmentation. Most projects today have a significant wicked component. Wicked problems are so commonplace that the chaos and futility that usually attend them are accepted as inevitable. Failing to recognize the 'wicked dynamics' in problems, we persist in applying inappropriate methods and tools to them.

Another force of fragmentation is *social complexity*, the number and diversity of players who are involved in a project. The more parties involved in a project, the more social complexity. The more diverse those parties are, the more social complexity. The fragmenting force of social complexity can make effective communication very difficult. Social complexity requires new understandings, processes, and tools that are attuned to the fundamentally *social* and *conversational* nature of work.

For example, in a joint project involving several companies and government agencies, there was a prolonged struggle over the mission statement simply because of a terminology difference: Each sponsoring agency had its own term for the core concept, and to pick one term meant disenfranchising one of the agencies. (The project concerned 'unmanned aerial vehicles,' also known as 'remotely piloted aircraft.') This is a very simple example of fragmentation of meaning.

Social complexity means that a project team works in a social network, a network of controllers and influencers including individual stakeholders, other project teams, and other organizations. These relationships, whether they are with direct stakeholders or those more peripherally involved, must be included in the project. For it is not whether the project team comes up with the right answer, but whose buy-in they have that really matters. To put it more starkly, without being included in the thinking and decision-making process, members of the social network may seek to undermine or even sabotage the project if their needs are not considered. Social complexity can be understood and used effectively, but it can be ignored only at great peril.

My janitor friend had an advantage over the rest of us in the organization because he could clearly see that his vacuum cleaner was not actually picking up the lint. When we are working on wicked problems in a socially complex environment, it is much harder to notice that our tools are simply not 'picking up the lint.'

As we enter the new millennium the forces of fragmentation appear to be increasing, and the increasing intensity of these forces causes more and more projects to flounder and fail. The bigger they are, the more intense the fragmenting forces, the more likely the projects are to fail. Or, to avoid outright failure, management will set the bar low ('we'll just convene a group and discuss the issue') or will cancel the project before the scheduled end, perhaps relaunching it under a different name.

Moreover, the situation is not that project teams are aware of fragmentation and are taking appropriate measures to deal with it – quite the opposite, most teams accept fragmentation as inevitable. Indeed, most people are unaware of some basic facts about novel and complex problems. Managers, in particular, seem to be unaware that linear processes are not effective with such problems.

Opportunity-Driven Problem Solving

A study in the 1980s at the Microelectronics and Computer Technology Corporation (MCC) looked into how people solve problems (Guindon, 1990). The study focused on design, but the results apply to virtually any other kind of problem solving or decision-making activity – the kinds projects are fraught with.

A number of designers participated in an experiment in which the exercise was to design an elevator control system for an office building. All the participants in the study were experienced and expert integrated circuit designers, but they had never worked on elevator systems before. Indeed, their only experience with elevator systems came from riding in elevators. Each participant was asked to think out loud while they worked on the problem. The sessions were video-taped and analyzed in great detail.

The analysis showed, not surprisingly, that these designers worked simultaneously on *understanding the problem* and *formulating a solution*. They exhibited two ways of trying to *understand the problem*:

- efforts to understand the requirements for the system (from a one-page problem statement they were given at the beginning of the session);
- mental simulations (e.g. 'Let's see, I'm on the second floor and the elevator is on the third floor and I push the "Up" button. That's going to create this situation.').

On the solution side, their activities were classified into *high*, *medium*, and *low* levels of design, with high-level design being general ideas, and low-level being details at the implementation level. These levels are analogous to an architect's sketch, working draw-ings, and a detailed blueprint and materials list for a house.

Traditional thinking, cognitive studies, and the prevailing design methods all predicted that the best way to work on a problem like this was to follow an orderly and linear 'top down' process, working from the problem to the solution. This logic is familiar to all of us. You begin by understanding the problem. This often includes gath-ering and analyzing 'requirements' from customers or users. Once you have the problem specified and the requirements analyzed, you are ready to formulate a solution, and eventually to implement that solution. This is illustrated by the 'waterfall' line in Figure 1.1.

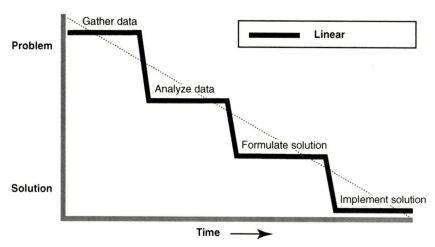

Figure 1.1   Traditional wisdom for solving complex problems: the 'waterfall'

This is the pattern of thinking that everyone attempts to follow when they are faced with a problem, and it is widely understood that the more complex the problem is, the more important it is to follow this orderly flow. If you work in a large organization, you will recognize this linear pattern as being enshrined in policy manuals, textbooks, internal standards for project management, and even the most advanced tools and methods being used and taught in the organization. In the software industry it is known as the 'waterfall model,' because it suggests the image of a waterfall as the project 'flows' down the steps towards completion.

However, the subjects in the elevator experiment did not follow a waterfall. They would start by trying to understand the problem, but they would immediately jump into formulating potential solutions. Then they would jump back up to refining their understanding of the problem. Rather than being orderly and linear, the line plotting the course of their thinking looks more like a seismograph for a major earthquake, as illustrated in Figure 1.2. We will refer to this jagged-line pattern as *opportunity driven*, because in each moment the designers are seeking the best opportunity for progress toward a solution.

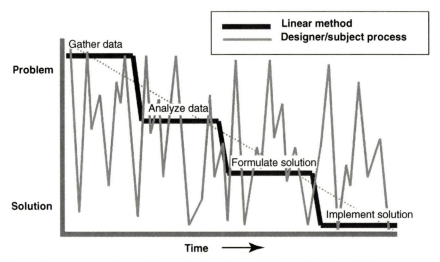

Figure 1.2   Pattern of cognitive activity of one designer: the 'jagged' line

These designers are not being irrational. They are not poorly trained or inexperienced. Their thought process was something like: 'Let's see, idle elevators should return to the first floor, but then, you only need one elevator on the first floor, so the others could move to an even distribution among the floors. But the elevators need to be vacuumed regularly. I suppose we could add a switch that brought idle elevators down to the first floor. But then what happens in an emergency?' In other words, what is driving the flow of thought is some marvelous internal drive to make the most headway possible, regardless of where the headway happens, by making *opportunity-driven* leaps in the focus of attention. It is precisely because these expert designers are being creative and because they are learning rapidly that the trace of their thinking pattern is full of unpredictable leaps.

In particular, the experiment showed that, faced with a novel and complex problem, human beings do not simply start by gathering and analyzing data about the problem. Cognition does not naturally form a pure and abstract understanding of 'the problem.' The subjects in the elevator experiment jumped immediately into thinking about what kind of processors to use in the elevator controller, and how to connect them, and how to deal with unexpected situations, such as if one processor failed. These are detailed solution elements.

These experienced designers illustrate that problem understanding can only come from creating possible solutions and considering how they might work. Indeed, the problem often can best be described in terms of solution elements. A requirement in the problem statement calling for 'high reliability' was quickly translated into the idea of using a network of distributed processors – a high-level solution that drove the rest of the design process.

Figure 1.2 illustrates another striking observation: problem understanding continues to evolve until the very end of the experiment. Even late in the experiments the subject designers returned to problem understanding, the upper part of the graph. Our experience in observing individuals and groups working on design and planning problems is that, indeed, their understanding of the problem continues to evolve – forever! Even well into the implementation of the design or plan, the understanding of the problem, the 'real issue,' is changing and growing.

The natural pattern of problem-solving behavior may appear chaotic on the surface, but it is the chaos of an earthquake or the breaking of an ocean wave – it reflects a deeper order in the cognitive process. The nonlinear pattern of activity that expert designers go through gives us fresh insight into what is happening when we are working on a complex and novel problem. It reveals that the feeling that we are 'wandering all over' is not a mark of stupidity or lack of training. This nonlinear process is not a defect, but rather the mark of an intelligent and creative learning process.

In fact, this nonlinear pattern does not come as a surprise to most people. Anyone who has ever worked on a complex project has the intuition that this jagged-line process is what is really going on. But the experiment is significant because it gives us an empirically grounded picture of the process that people follow when they really think about novel problems, and it is not the orderly and linear process we have been taught is proper!

From another perspective, the jagged line of opportunity-driven problem solving is a picture of *learning*. The more novel the problem, the more the problem-solving process involves learning about the *problem domain*. In this sense, the waterfall is a picture of already knowing – you already know about the problem and its domain, you know about the right process and tools to solve it, and you know what a solution will look like. As much as we might wish it were otherwise, most projects in the knowledge economy operate much more in the realm of learning than already knowing. You still have experts, but it's no longer possible for them to guide the project down the linear waterfall process. In the current business environment, problem solving and learning are tightly intertwined, and the flow of this learning process is opportunity driven.

Some readers might object to this claim. Perhaps most folks in their organization have a strong sense of certainty about what is going on, a sense of confidence and pride in their knowledge of their business, and a sense that the problems the business is confronted with are quite manageable using the methodical application of well-known rules and linear process logic. To these readers let me just say, 'Congratulations!' Certainly not all of the modern economy is knowledge based, not all problems are wicked, and there are many who still enjoy a sense of quiet confidence and control in their professional lives. This book is not for them.

If your organization is a professional or consulting services business, or if there is a large technology component (including the Internet) to your organization's products or business process, then you are all too familiar with the roller coaster ride of opportunity-driven problem solving. There are many reasons for this state of affairs, but one of the most important is that *you are operating in the realm of a special kind of problem: the wicked problem.* Wicked problems are one of the fragmenting forces mentioned at the beginning of this chapter, and it essential to understand the properties of wicked problems in order to counter and manage their fragmenting impact on projects.

Wicked Problems

The man who coined the term 'wicked problem,' Horst Rittel, was also the inventor of the issue-based information system (IBIS) structure on which dialogue mapping is based (Rittel, 1972a; Rittel and Webber, 1973). Rittel and his colleagues perceived the limitations of the linear 'systems approach' of design and planning over 30 years ago, and their research provides a foundation for what Rittel termed a 'second generation' of systems analysis methodology. Rittel invented IBIS because, as an urban planner and designer, he found traditional planning methods inadequate for the ill-structured problems he encountered in city planning.

Rittel's genius shines especially bright when we consider his solution for wicked problems: IBIS, a structure for rational *dialogue* among a set of diverse stakeholders. This is a perspective that puts human relationships and social interactions at the center, a perspective that is only now coming into vogue as a key insight of post-modern thought.

As Rittel defined them,[1] wicked problems are distinguished by the following characteristics:

1 *You don't understand the problem until you have developed a solution.* Every solution that is offered exposes new aspects of the problem, requiring further adjustments of the potential solutions. Indeed, there is no definitive statement of 'the problem.' The problem is ill structured, an evolving set of interlocking issues and constraints. Rittel said: 'One cannot understand the problem without knowing about its context; one cannot meaningfully search for information without the orientation of a solution concept; one cannot first understand, then solve.' Moreover, what 'the problem' is depends on who you ask – different stakeholders have different views about what the problem is and what constitutes an acceptable solution.[2]

2 *Wicked problems have no stopping rule.* Since there is no definitive 'the problem,' there is also no definitive 'the solution.' The problem-solving process ends when you run out of resources, such as time, money, or energy, not when some optimal or 'final and correct' solution emerges. Herb Simon, Nobel laureate in economics, called this 'satisficing' – stopping when you have a solution that is 'good enough' (Simon, 1969).

3   *Solutions to wicked problems are not right or wrong.* They are simply 'better,' 'worse,' 'good enough,' or 'not good enough.' With wicked problems, the determination of solution quality is not objective and cannot be derived from following a formula. Solutions are assessed in a social context in which 'many parties are equally equipped, interested, and/or entitled to judge [them],' and these judgements are likely to vary widely and depend on the stakeholder's independent values and goals.

4   *Every wicked problem is essentially unique and novel.* There are so many factors and conditions, all embedded in a dynamic social context, that no two wicked problems are alike, and the solutions to them will always be custom designed and fitted. Rittel said: 'The condition in a city constructing a subway may look similar to the conditions in San Francisco, say, . . . but differences in commuter habits or residential patterns may far outweigh similarities in subway layout, downtown layout, and the rest.' Over time one acquires wisdom and experience about the approach to wicked problems, but one is always a beginner in the specifics of a new wicked problem.

5   *Every solution to a wicked problem is a 'one-shot operation.'* Every attempt has consequences. As Rittel says: 'One cannot build a freeway to see how it works.' This is the 'Catch 22' about wicked problems: you can't learn about the problem without trying solutions, but every solution you try is expensive and has lasting unintended consequences which are likely to spawn new wicked problems.

6   *Wicked problems have no given alternative solutions.* There may be no solutions, or there may be a host of potential solutions that are devised, and another host that are never even thought of. Thus, it is a matter of *creativity* to devise potential solutions, and a matter of *judgement* to determine which are valid, which should be pursued and implemented.

These criteria are more descriptive than definitional. The point is not so much to be able to determine if a given problem is wicked or not as to have a sense of what contributes to the 'wickedness' of a problem.

Here are a few examples of wicked problems:

- Route the highway through our city or around it?
- How to deal with crime and violence in our schools?
- What to do when oil resources run out?
- What should our mission statement be?
- What features should be in our new product?

While many of the problems that we will look at in this chapter are problems that occur in organizations, the above list should make it clear that many of the social problems that we face in our communities are also 'wicked problems.'

Wicked Problem Example: a New Car Design

Let's consider a potentially wicked problem in the design of a new car. Let's imagine a project team that has formed around a new assignment: the marketing department is asking for a design that emphasizes side-impact safety – they want to promote a new 'safe car' to compete with Volvo. That is the problem to be solved, that is the work of the project. There is a deadline and a budget and a senior executive that the project reports to.

Now consider the criteria for a wicked problem again:

1 *You don't understand the problem until you have developed a solution.* One approach to making a safer car would be to add structural support in the doors to make the car safer from side

impact. It turns out that the additional door structure doubles the cost of the door, makes the doors heavier and harder to open and close, changes the fuel mileage and ride, and requires an adjustment to the suspension and braking systems. Making the doors stronger leads into other design problems, but also bounces back into marketing problems such as 'What should the price be?', 'How much do people really care about side impact survivability?', 'What do customers really want in a car?' All of these problems interact with each other. And at the senior executive level, the real question is 'Should we continue this project to produce this new car?'

2 *Wicked problems have no stopping rule.* When does the car become 'safe'? There is no natural stopping point in working out the tradeoffs among safety, performance, appearance, and cost. At some point, the design team will be forced to make a decision. If it were not for project deadlines, the team would swirl indefinitely in 'analysis paralysis.'

3 *Solutions to wicked problems are not right or wrong.* No amount of study, laboratory experiments, or market surveys will establish that that project team's solution is 'correct.' Ironically, when the car gets produced, there will be reviews pointing out that the doors are heavy and difficult to open when parking on a hill, mixed with lawsuits from people who were injured in side-impact accidents despite the stronger doors.

4 *Every wicked problem is essentially unique and novel.* Even if the project team has several successful car designs under its belt, the 'safe door' problem is essentially unique and novel, because of the configuration of issues and stakeholders. First, a recent study by a consumer safety organization suggests that side-impact injuries would be reduced by side airbags, which are not a part of the design. Second, a side-impact injury lawsuit has been filed against the company – if the new design is announced now, it may

look like an acknowledgement of prior unsafe designs. Moreover, federal legislation is emerging that may put legal constraints on the strength of the doors. The design of safer doors is not merely a technical problem: It is a political and PR problem as well.

5 *Every solution to a wicked problem is a 'one-shot operation.'* The creation of a safer car is a one-shot operation. When the new safer car finally reaches the market, it may be a flop, or it may change the safety standards for the whole industry. The design team can build prototypes of the car and test them, but there is no way to anticipate the unintended consequences of producing and selling the new vehicle.

6 *Wicked problems have no given alternative solutions.* The safe door problem does not have a few discrete possible solutions from which to choose. There is an immense space of options in terms of structural reinforcement, materials, cushioning, window design, hinge placement, and how the door latches and opens. The design team cannot select from a few options – it must collectively exercise creativity and judgement about an elegant resolution of all the design priorities.

The design of a new 'safe car' is an example of a wicked problem. It cannot be solved by engineers alone, neither is there any way of determining that any given solution is 'correct' or even optimal. It all depends on where you stand.

Coping with Wicked Problems

Not all problems are wicked. In contrast, a *'tame problem'* is one for which the traditional linear process is sufficient to produce a workable solution in an acceptable time frame. A tame problem:

1 has a well-defined and stable problem statement;
2 has a definite stopping point, i.e. when the solution is reached;

3   has a solution that can be objectively evaluated as right or wrong;
4   belongs to a class of similar problems that are all solved in the same similar way;
5   has solutions that can be easily tried and abandoned;
6   comes with a limited set of alternative solutions.

Finding the square root of 7358 is a tame problem, as is finding the shortest route from A to B on a map. Repairing a computer, raising $10000, and selecting a new doctor when you move to a new city are all tame, if complex and difficult, problems. Tame does not mean simple – a tame problem can be technically very complex.

A problem doesn't have to possess all six characteristics in order to be wicked. Putting a man on the moon was a problem with a lot of wickedness, for example, but also with some tame elements. There were certainly some wicked sub-problems. But notice that the main problem statement, putting a man on the moon and returning him safely, did not change over time (criterion 1). There was a definite 'stopping point' at which we could say we had solved that problem (criterion 2). And the solution could be clearly evaluated as having succeeded or failed (criterion 3). It may be convenient to describe a problem as wicked or tame, but it's not binary – most problems have degrees of wickedness.

You also can't tell from the outside if a problem is going to be wicked. Like the safe car design example, many problems appear tame on the surface, but are indeed wicked once you get into them.

The first step in coping with a wicked problem is to recognize its nature. There is a tendency to treat all problems as tame, perhaps because tame problems are easier to solve, reinforced by the lack of understanding about wicked problem dynamics and the tools and approach they require. There is a psychological dimension here – a shift from denial to acceptance.

The command and control paradigm of management reinforces blindness about the true nature of the problem. Inherent in this paradigm is the idea that a person in charge gives the solution (the right solution, the only solution) to other people, who are in charge of implementing it. To function in such a hierarchy often means to collude in systematic denial of the complex and ill-structured dynamics of wicked problems, a phenomenon dubbed 'skilled incompetence' by Chris Argyris (e.g. Argyris and Schön, 1996).

As a result, there are two common organizational coping mechanisms that are routinely applied to wicked problems: *studying* the problem, and *taming* it.

While studying a novel and complex problem is natural and important, it is an approach that will run out of gas quickly if the problem is wicked. Pure study amounts to procrastination, because little can be learned about a wicked problem by objective data gathering and analysis. Wicked problems demand an opportunity-driven approach; they require making decisions, doing experiments, launching pilot programs, testing prototypes, and so on. Study alone leads to more study, and results in the condition known as 'analysis paralysis,' a Catch 22 in which we can't take action until we have more information, but we can't get more information until someone takes action. One corporation I worked with, struggling to decide between two very different strategic paths for the future, studied and discussed the two options for so long that, by the time they had decided and implemented their choice, the chosen option was no longer viable.

Taming a wicked problem is a very natural and common way of coping with it. Instead of dealing with the full wickedness of the problem, one simplifies it in various ways to make it more manageable – to make it solvable! There are (at least) six ways to tame wicked problems, corresponding to the six criteria for wickedness:

1   *Lock down the problem definition.* Develop a description of a related problem or a sub-problem that you *can* solve, and declare that to be the problem. Resist all efforts to expand or modify the problem definition. For example, if the problem is how to reduce violence in schools, you could focus on the much more tractable problem of how to install metal detectors in all school entrances. As another example, in the software field, one learns to 'freeze the requirements,' or to put them in a legally binding document, as a way to lock down the problem.

2   *Assert that the problem is solved.* Since a wicked problem has no definitive solution, the whole point of attempting to tame it is so that a solution can be reached. Usually this step requires locking the problem down (see point 1), although it is possible to simply assert that the problem is 'solved' without clarity about what the problem was. Such assertions, however, generally require considerable authority to appear successful, such as in an autocratic organization or a dictatorship. As an example illustrates, one way of dealing with a United Nations resolution demanding that you destroy all weapons of mass destruction in your country is to simply assert that you have done so. It should be clear that this approach to taming a problem depends critically on how compelling your case is that the problem is solved.

3   *Specify objective parameters by which to measure the solution's success.* This is the measurement approach. For example, to find out if we have solved the problem of school violence, we might

count the number of deaths and injuries on school property – if this measure drops to zero, then we have solved the problem. This taming approach amounts to locking the problem down (point 1), however, because what is measured becomes, officially and by definition, the problem. Whatever is not measured is then free to absorb the real problem. With intense enough focus, we might reduce the number of violent incidents on the school grounds to zero . . . problem solved! . . . but overlook new problems that had been created, such as a sharp rise in violent incidents just off the school grounds.

4   *Cast the problem as 'just like' a previous problem that has been solved.* Ignore or filter out evidence that complicates the picture. Refer to the previous solution of the related problem: 'It's just like that problem. Just do the same thing again.' For example, there is a saying in military circles that 'we always fight the last war,' meaning the tendency to assume that the enemy will behave as he did in the last war.

5   *Give up on trying to get a good solution to the problem.* Just follow orders, do your job, and try not to get in trouble. Maybe the organization will fix the serious shortcomings of the current solution in a revised version or release next year.

6   *Declare that there are just a few possible solutions, and focus on selecting from among these options.* A specific way to do this is to frame the problem in 'either/or' terms, e.g. 'Should we attack Iraq or let the terrorists take over the world?'

Different people prefer different coping mechanisms – some would rather study the problem until they really understand it; others, impatient with sitting around, would rather tame the problem to something manageable and jump into action. However, attempting to tame a wicked problem, while appealing in the short run, fails in the long run. The wicked problem simply reasserts itself, perhaps in a different guise, as if nothing had been done. Or, worse, sometimes the tame solution exacerbates the problem.

Social Complexity

At the beginning of the chapter we asserted that the two most intensely fragmenting forces impacting projects today are wicked problems and social complexity. These forces tend to co-occur. Can a socially complex group have a tame problem? Probably so. Can an individual have a wicked problem? Yes, according to Rittel's definition. Yet the concepts are distinct: while wickedness is a property of the problem/solution space and the cognitive dynamics of exploring that space, social complexity is a property of the social network that is engaging with the problem.

Social complexity is a function of the number and diversity of players who are involved in a project. The more parties involved in a project, the more social complexity. The more diverse those parties are, the more social complexity.

Projects and problem solving have always been social in nature. Project success has always depended on collaborative skills and collective intelligence. But in earlier times of greater social homogeneity, the collaborative skills picked up in the playground were sufficient. The rules of engagement of family dynamics held in project meetings, and hierarchical authority could always be used to sort out the hardest parts. Now, in the 'knowledge workforce,' more democratic models of decision making are being used. Also, women have a far stronger role, often playing leadership roles. Minorities and foreign nationals are often present on the team. The old assumption that 'we all pretty much think and act the same way' just doesn't hold any more. In addition, organizations are flattening, opening up, and moving toward increased workplace democracy. More disciplines, departments, and dogmas are represented on the typical project team. This diversity is important for the wider space of options and considerations in play, which in turn leads to creative solutions that are more durable and robust. But it also presents new process and leadership challenges.

The jagged line graph from the MCC elevator study can help us visualize the impact of social complexity on a project. Imagine adding a second designer, represented by the dotted line in Figure 1.3, to help solve the elevator design problem.

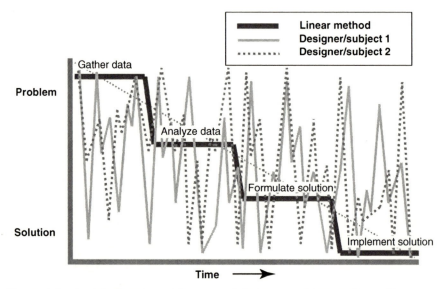

Figure 1.3 A wicked project with a second designer working on the problem

Notice that the second designer, like the first designer, goes through an opportunity-driven process between the problem and solution spaces, but the new designer's thinking process is quite different in the particulars from the first designer's. Since she has a different background and training, the pattern of her cognitive flow will also differ.

Let's imagine you are the project leader. You are the one who is responsible for the project being on time, in budget, and meeting all its requirements. Even if you understand that the process is going to be opportunity driven, you must still make plans, create schedules, allocate resources, and commit to milestones. You can't 'plan' for the process to be opportunity driven! Thus, in effect, you are officially in charge of keeping the project on the waterfall line.

Now let's consider two project team meetings, occurring at different points along the time line. At meeting A in Figure 1.4, you are a happy project leader because everyone is in synch, focused on the same activity, analyzing the requirements just like it says in 'the book.' Your prospects for bringing your project in on time and in budget look good.

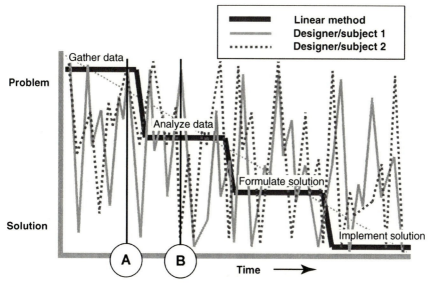

Figure 1.4 Two team meetings, A and B, during the project

Some time later, at meeting B in Figure 1.4, the team has finished up with the data analysis and is now in the next phase, high-level design. But there are signs of trouble. Designer 1 looks tired but radiant. He says, 'I was driving home last night and I had an idea. I stayed up all night programming, and . . . you won't believe this, but . . . I put together a program that does the whole thing. Sure, it still needs a little work, but, hey, we're practically done! Way ahead of schedule! I can't wait to show it to you!' In his personal opportunity-driven process, he has made a major leap, all the way to the bottom of the chart, to the final solution.

There is a long pause. Designer 2 also looks tired, but not so radiant. Holding up the long-finished requirements document she says, 'Sorry, we're not even *close* to done. I was with the client yesterday, and it turns out that there is a set of transactions that the system needs to handle that they never even told us about. Six months ago they said it didn't have anything to do with our project. But it turns out it has a *lot* to do with our system. We've got to go back to square one and start over!'

Neither of these key players is where you need them to be, according to the linear plan you created at the beginning of the project. You can feel chaos rising and control slipping away. You desperately plead with them to refocus on the high-level design, because, according to the calendar, that's where the project needs to be.

Perhaps you turn to the first designer and say something like, 'That's a good idea, Henry – but we really need to finish the high-level design. Can you hang on to that code for a while?' Turning to the other designer, you beg, 'Look Sally, we already have gotten those requirements signed off. We can't go back. We'll just have to take care of those new transactions in the next release of the system.'

This scenario exemplifies a tiny slice of the tension that is inherently part of working in a socially complex environment. Despite the most carefully thought-out plans, wicked problem dynamics and the diversity of jobs and orientations fragment the project team and its process. The above scenario is mild – there are only three stakeholders involved in the project. As projects grow in size and organizations grow flatter, social complexity increases. Large projects typically have dozens of stakeholders, representing the project team, other departments, and other organizations. And not only do all have their own 'jagged line,' they are likely to have different ideas about what the real issues are, and what the criteria for success are.

Consider the safe car design team. Bob, from Marketing, has been conducting studies and focus groups that indicate a lot of interest in cars that are safer in a collision. He is concerned with how to package a new 'safe car' in a way that is positive, sexy, and upbeat. Christine, from Engineering, is very concerned about making the doors too heavy, but she has worked on structural integrity in the past and is excited about new technologies that, while expensive, could make the doors both stronger and lighter. Harry, the representative from the Management Team, sees the big issue as cost – top management is pushing affordability and value as the new strategy to increase sales. Alan, from IT, has a mandate from his management to get this team to use the new CAD (computer-aided design) system on this project. There are team members who represent Regulatory Affairs, Finance, Graphic Design, Power Train, and Quality Assurance, as well as team members from several major suppliers, including electronics and interior materials.

Each player has their own individual experience, personality type, and style of thinking and learning. Each player adds a new jagged line to the graph. The individual diversity among these players will make collective intelligence a challenge, and will make consensus virtually impossible to achieve.

But social complexity doesn't stop with individual diversity – each of these players comes from a different *discipline*, with its own specialized language and culture. When Bob is among his colleagues in Marketing, they share a common body of knowledge, a common set of concerns and distinctions, and shared ways of thinking about and dealing with those concerns. However, when Bob tries to talk to Christine, from Engineering, he finds that she has little knowledge of basic marketing concepts, and seems to be uninterested in them. It's as if she were from a different country, speaking a different language. Thus, achieving shared meaning and shared context is especially difficult.

Moreover, social complexity goes beyond individual diversity and diversity among disciplines. The real corker is that these players represent different *organizations*. Each organization has its own function and charter, its own goals, and is managed by its own executive director. These organizations often have divergent goals. Marketing is trying to make its sales numbers, while Engineering is trying to win the Baldridge quality award. When the members of a project team come together to collaborate, they represent not only themselves but also their respective management chain in the hierarchy. Ideally, everyone in the organization is committed to the same thing, but, operationally, goals and agendas can be quite fragmented.

Thus, social complexity makes wicked problems even more wicked, raising the bar of collaborative success higher than ever.

Let's revisit the criteria for wicked problems for a moment. The main feature of a wicked problem is that you don't understand the problem until you have a solution. But with social complexity, 'not under-standing the problem' does not show up as innocent wonder about the mystery of the problem, neither does it usually occur as a thoughtful collective inquiry into the deeper nature of the problem.

Rather, 'not understanding the problem' shows up as different stakeholders who are certain that *their* version of the problem is correct or at least that other versions are fatally flawed. In severe cases, such as many political situations, each stakeholder's position about what the problem is reflects the mission and objectives of the organization (or country) they represent. In such cases there is a fine line between collaboration and colluding with the enemy. How can you make headway on a mutually acceptable solution if the stake-holders cannot agree on what the problem is?

The answer to this question – and the Holy Grail of effective collab-oration – is in *creating shared understanding about the problem, and shared commitment to the possible solutions.* Shared understanding does not mean we necessarily *agree* on the problem, although that is a good thing when it happens. Shared understanding means that the stakeholders understand each other's positions well enough to have intelligent dialogue about the different interpretations of the problem, and to exercise collective intelligence about how to solve it.

Because of social complexity, solving a wicked problem is *funda-mentally a social process*. Having a few brilliant people or the latest project management technology is no longer sufficient.

This book offers a practical approach for creating shared under-standing and shared commitment in a complex social network, and explores the underlying principles that make this approach effective. But before we can get into the 'solution' offered in this book, we need to consider a few more pieces of the collaborative puzzle that is posed by wicked problems and social complexity.

Design Polarity

Most projects wrestle with large social networks and their attendant complexity. It would be a mistake, however, to think that small project teams can escape fragmentation. Design possesses a fundamental property that can make a team of *two* socially complex. All that is needed is a representative from each of the two polarities of design: what is needed (marketing), and what can be built (engineering).

Virtually all creative work is a process of *design*. To design simply means 'to formulate a plan for,' 'to plan out in systematic, usually graphic form,' and 'to create or contrive for a particular purpose or effect' (American Heritage Dictionary, 2000). All problems call for *designing* a solution. All projects are essentially *designing* something. Design, in both the technical and artistic sense, is the process of creating something new – e.g., a new car, a strategic plan, a software program, a stickier website, next year's budget, a new environmental policy.

Any design problem is a problem of resolving tension between what is needed and what can be done. On the one hand, the process of design is driven by some desire or need – someone wants or needs something new. The need might be expressed by a customer, or it may be a guess about what the market wants. The need or want is expressed in the language of what *ought to be* – what should be done, what should be built, what should be written. On the other hand, the process of design is constrained by resources – what *can be done* given the available resources such as time and money and the constraints imposed by the environment and the laws of physics.

Every need has a price tag – the process of design is about devising solutions that are feasible and cost effective. Going back to the safe car design, the need might be quite specific, e.g., the car must protect the occupants from harm if it is struck from the side by another vehicle of similar weight traveling at 30 miles an hour. It may turn out that such a car would cost twice as much as a normally safe car. It may turn out to be impossible at *any* cost. Perhaps we have to change the need: reduce the required speed of safe impact to 10 miles an hour, because then it only increases the cost of the car by 15%.

Thus, in a very basic way, every project is about reconciling the fundamental polarity between the world of what-is-needed and the world of what-can-be-done. These two worlds correspond to the upper and lower halves of the MCC elevator study diagram. In Figure 1.5, the

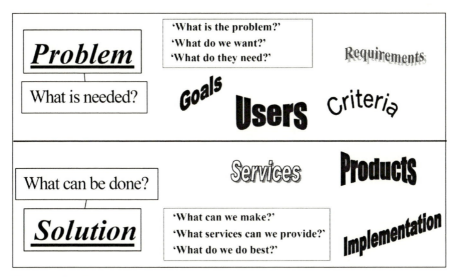

Figure 1.5   The two parts of the world of design

upper half, being about understanding the problem, is focused out in the world on a specific client or user or market. There is always someone who has a need or a desire, and the task in the problem or what-is-needed aspect of design is to specify that need. The lower half, being about the solution, is focused 'in the shop' on what-can-be-built – what do we have the resources and skills and tools to actually make, and what will it cost and how long will it take. (The object of design is not necessarily physical; one can design a plan, a budget, or a new mission statement.)

As you can see, there is an immense difference between these two worlds. When an individual does design, she stands with one foot in each world. Moving back and forth between the two worlds, she tries to create a solution that joins the two polarities of design in an elegant way. Design teams have a bigger challenge. While it is possible for each person on a project team to be standing in both worlds, the tendency is for the polarity of design to be reflected in a polarity of roles. The world of what-is-needed is the domain of the marketing and sales department, and sometimes upper management, whereas the world of what-can-be-done is territory that belongs to the engineering (or manufacturing, software development, IT, etc.) department.

The inherent unity of the design process turns into a battle between departments. The world of what-is-needed, claimed by the marketing department, becomes a self-referential world with its own culture and customs and language. The world of what-can-be-done is claimed by the technologists, the nerds and hackers who actually build things, with its own culture and customs and language. When they sit down together on a project, the polarity of design turns into an intercultural war that is expensive, wasteful, and ineffective, a war frequently featured in Scott Adams' 'Dilbert' cartoons.

Thus social complexity is not just a function of the *number* of stakeholders – it is also a function of structural relationships among the stakeholders. While large projects have an increasing number and diversity of stakeholders, it only takes one player from each side of the polarity of design – one from marketing and one from engineering – to cause the collaborative gears to grind to a halt.

Technical Complexity

In addition to wicked problems and social complexity, technical complexity is a potentially fragmenting force. Technical complexity includes the number of technologies that are involved in a project, the immense number of possible interactions among them, and the rate of technical change. For example, to be a serious player in the software industry today, your software must run on a variety of types of computer. Each type (or 'platform') has several operating systems, and each operating system has many versions that are currently in the field and must be supported. You must choose what language your software will be written in: Java, C, C++, Cobol, Fortran, etc. Each of these programming languages has a variety of supported versions (compilers); for example, Microsoft and Sun each has a major version of the popular Java language used in World Wide Web applications. Then you must choose the set of utilities ('library') you will use for creating your user interface. There are dozens of other choices, and all these options interact with each other. Moreover, the field is changing so fast that new options become available, and others drop into oblivion, almost every day.

As much as technical complexity raises the risk of project failure, it is also the best-recognized fragmenting force. So much has been written about technical complexity and how to deal with it, so many tools and methods are available, that there is little to add here. The dialogue mapping approach presented in this book excels at dealing with complex technical information, but the real power of dialogue mapping, and the point of this book, is to provide an approach and a set of tools for dealing with the nontechnical side of fragmentation: wicked problem dynamics and social complexity.

Fragmentation and Coherence

We have described wicked problems, social complexity, and technical complexity as forces that fragment projects, causing them to fail. It is important to recognize that these forces are not due to incompetence, poor management, or any human failing. They are part of the 'physics' of a project. There is no quick fix for the phenomenon of wicked problems. No glib formula about 'seven steps to crush social complexity' or 'tame your way to the top.'

Moreover, the physics of fragmentation is obscured by a cultural condition of resignation, denial, and grim determination that has grown up around it. In my consulting and facilitation experience I have met this condition over and over in organizations and on project teams. I have seen it manifest in many forms, sometimes as outright panic, sometimes as plodding determination, sometimes as a vague sense of futility. This condition of organizational pain is so chronic, however, that, like low-grade back pain, it has faded into the background of organizational experience and is taken for granted, assumed to be normal and inevitable. The condition is not wicked problems, or social complexity – these are causes of the condition.

Once this chronic condition is seen and understood, in my experience, then compassion can emerge for what we are up against when we go to work. For what we *do* accomplish and the courage that it takes. A whole new perspective about work and life opens up.

This is why it is so useful to distinguish the common element of fragmentation. Wicked problems fragment the process of project work, especially when the problem is misdiagnosed as tame. Wicked problems also fragment direction and mission – if you can't agree on what the problem is how can you be aligned on a solution? Social complexity fragments team identity – the ideal of team unity is compromised by the dynamics of competing interests and hidden agendas. The duality of design tends to divide allegiances between requirements and implementation. Social complexity also fragments meaning – key terms and concepts are used in different ways by the different stakeholders. Project teams are often geographically distributed, further fragmenting relationships and communications. Participants in a modern project team are pulled in a thousand different directions by the centrifugal forces of wicked problems, social complexity, and technical complexity (see Figure 1.6).

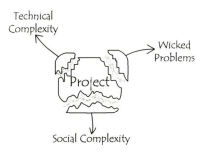

Figure 1.6 'Centrifugal' fragmenting forces pulling a project apart

The notion of fragmentation points to all of these problems, but it is pretty abstract. Because it points deep into the culture and practices of project work, it is difficult to observe fragmentation directly. There is, however, a more observable indicator of fragmentation: *blame*. Instead of seeing the systemic nature of project challenges and the value of social diversity, we tend to see a big mess, to view it as the result of incompetence, and to blame each other for it. We blame upper management for sending mixed signals or for lack of direction. We blame HR for poor hiring practices and lack of training. We blame the 'bean counters' for over-tight budgets and lack of fiscal flexibility. We blame IT for confusion and the lack of stable infrastructure. We blame our customers for not knowing what they really want. We blame each other because we have different personalities and learning styles. (How many conversations do you notice in your organization that involve placing blame?)

In times of stress the natural human tendency is to find fault with someone else. People tend to take a wicked problem 'personally,' at an organizational level, and assume that the chaos they see is a result of incompetence or, worse, insincere leadership. Since their education and experience have prepared them to see and solve tame problems, wicked problems sneak up on them and create chaos. Without understanding the 'wickedness' of the situation, there is finger pointing instead of learning.

Not so long ago most human illness was regarded as the result of evil spirits, so, when people got sick, the fix was to let the evil spirits out, for example by drilling holes in their heads. It wasn't very effective, but – within that system of thought – it was rational. These days, when big projects run into problems, we hold emergency meetings, then fire the consultants or rearrange the org chart. It isn't very effective, but it's a rational response to fragmentation . . . *if* you believe that the problems result from human failing, i.e. poor performance or incompetence.

I was doing some training with a management team at a utility company several years ago. The human resources (HR) department had recently announced a new policy regarding the way employee performance would be evaluated and reported in the future, and these managers were very upset because the policy was so obviously flawed, and it had a direct impact on them. 'What were they thinking?!?' and 'Those morons in HR!' they exclaimed. As an exercise we decided to design a better policy. After an hour and a half we reviewed our solutions, and what do you suppose they realized? That it was a very hard problem, given the organizational and legal constraints in the system, and that, all things considered, HR had come up with a pretty good approach! They shifted from blame to deeper understanding of the problem.

If we step back and take a systemic view, we can see that the issue is not whose fault the mess is – the issue is our collective failure to recognize the recurring and inevitable dynamics of the mess. If we take a systemic view, we turn away from blame and away from easy technical fixes, and look in the social domain – in building capacity to collaborate effectively on wicked problems.

As Rittel said: 'We are now sensitized to the waves of repercussions generated by a problem-solving decision directed to any one node in the network, and we are no longer surprised to find it inducing problems of greater severity at some other node' (Rittel and Webber, 1973; see also the 'Disturbing Complexity' chapters of Pascal, Millemann & Gioja, 2000).

The antidote for fragmentation is coherence. How, then, do we create coherence? In organizations and project teams – in situations where collaboration is the lifeblood of success – coherence amounts to shared understanding and shared commitment. Shared understanding of meaning and context, and of the dimensions and issues in the problem. Shared commitment to the processes of project work and to the emergent solution matrix.

Coherence means that stakeholders have shared meaning for key terms and concepts, that they are clear about their role in the effort, that together they have a shared understanding of the background for the project and what the issues are, and that they have a shared commitment to how the project will reach its objectives and achieve success. Coherence means that the project team understands and is aligned with the goals of the project and how to reach them. Coherence means that a wicked problem is recognized as such, and appropriate tools and processes are constantly used to 'defragment' the project. With increased coherence, more collective intelligence becomes available to deal with change and complexity. Coherence means that despite social complexity there is a sense of ability and confidence in crafting shared understanding and negotiating shared meaning.

Notes

1. Rittel had a more exhaustive list of 10 criteria for wicked problems (Rittel and Webber, 1973). I have attempted to simplify the concept somewhat without losing its essence.
2. Wicked problems pose a terminology dilemma. There is no 'the problem' in the traditional sense – like Heisenberg's elementary particles, getting close enough to the problem to see it . . . changes it. Similarly, no 'solution' is ever achieved, in the traditional sense. We might better use terms

like 'domain of concerns and needs' for 'problem', and 'domain of resolution and satisfaction' for 'solution.' However, for expediency and clarity, we will use the more familiar terms. So when we say 'developed a solution' we don't mean a final, mutually acceptable solution, we simply mean a proposal that might resolve some part or aspect of a wicked problem.

Summary

This chapter has been about laying a foundation that identifies the 'problem' that dialogue mapping addresses. This problem is:

- the powerful fragmenting forces of wicked problems, social complexity, and technical complexity;
- the confusion, chaos, and blame created by failing to distinguish these forces;
- the lack of tools and techniques for 'defragmenting' project dynamics.

The process of dialogue mapping is a powerful approach for addressing the problem of fragmentation, as it allows a diverse group of people to generate coherence around wicked problems. This group coherence is a necessary step toward addressing fragmentation, yet it is neither a silver bullet nor a cure-all. Given the complex nature of organizations, it is not sufficient for a single team or even multiple teams to achieve coherence; the organization as a whole needs to become a knowledge organization, and gain a kind of 'literacy' or 'fluency' in the language of coherence: distinctions, tools, methods, and practices for crafting shared understanding and shared commitment. Dialogue mapping is a practical first step toward that kind of literacy because it targets meetings, where most project communication takes place, and where fragmentation plays out most dramatically.

In the next chapter we explore the physics of coherence, and in particular the marvelously cohering forces of *shared understanding* and *shared commitment*. Following that, in Chapter 3, we shift gears and peek in on a dialogue mapping session.

2
Building Shared Understanding

If projects are beset with fragmenting forces due to wicked problems and social complexity, the question becomes: how to create coherence with equally strong anti-fragmentation forces?

Project fragmentation takes many forms and has many sources; similarly, there are many ways to create coherence. The whole domain of project management, for example – of practices dealing with planning, resource allocation, and scheduling – serves to create coherence in a project. Hiring, retention, management and leadership, vendor relations, contract law, subcontractor management . . . all have their own tools, skills, and practices that help to make projects successful. However, none of these disciplines, no matter how expertly done, can create clarity and commitment among diverse stakeholders. You can't schedule consensus between groups competing for scarce resources, neither can you make robust decisions by management fiat. The only way to lubricate the wheels and gears of the social network is by attending to the social dimension of project work and finding ways to build shared understanding about the project situation – about the dimensions of the problem and the constraints and criteria for possible solutions.

Shared understanding is not the same as consensus. It does not mean everybody agrees with each other. Shared understanding among stakeholders in a project means that the stakeholders know about each others' concerns and goals. They have had enough social contact that there is some modicum of trust and caring among them. They have forged shared meaning about critical terms and concepts. They have interacted with each other enough that a collective sense of 'we-ness' has begun to emerge – where we came from, what we are trying to do, what we have accomplished so far. Shared understanding often includes agreement about what is *not* agreed on and what is *not* known yet.

So, how do you build shared understanding?

You begin by augmenting the 'container' for meetings – vastly increasing the capacity for dealing with massive amounts of information, strongly held opinions, factual incongruities, difficult personalities, and divergent goals and priorities.[1]

Meetings are the natural starting point for creating shared understanding, because meetings are the communication hubs of projects. Meetings are where knowledge gets created, decisions are made, ideas are surfaced and promoted, actions are assigned, and issues are sorted out. Meetings are the veins and arteries of the social network – they are where relationships develop, where coalitions and alliances are created, and where power is brokered. Meetings are also where fragmentation shows up most clearly, where the collaborative pain throbs most intensely, and they are thus the natural starting point for defragmenting the project.

Clearly, not all project collaboration happens in formal meetings. A lot of collaborative work occurs in hallways and restaurants, on the phone, in documents, and in email. Project team members who are working alone at their computer building a model or a report are collaborating implicitly. The dialogue mapping approach extends to distributed teams, online discussions, and virtual meetings, but in my experience you must start where the white heat of collaborative action and its attendant breakdowns are happening: in the meeting room.

In addition to shared understanding, project coherence is also built on *shared commitment* to the project's direction and goals, the emerging solutions, group decisions, and the actions needed to keep the project moving forward. Shared commitment is about decisions that stick and promises that get kept. Shared commitment is another force of coherence, like shared understanding. The difference is that shared understanding focuses on where we are, shared commitment focuses on where we're going. In years of working with all kinds of different groups, I have seen over and over again that, if shared understanding is deep enough and rich enough, shared commitment emerges naturally.

Dialogue mapping (defined below) is a way to support collective intelligence through building shared understanding and shared commitment. The 'magic trick' of dialogue mapping, if you will, is to create a 'shared display' that incorporates each person's contribution to the sense-making process.

Recall the jagged-line pattern of opportunity-driven problem solving in Figure 1.2 (page 10). Dialogue mapping has the flexibility needed to track and organize the whole spectrum of insights and information from problem to solution. Shared understanding is inherently nurtured as the group sees its collective thinking – questions, concerns, ideas, decisions, assumptions, and so on – rendered in issue-based 'maps' that grow as the dialogue unfolds. No problem is too wicked, no social network too diverse, that these living maps cannot foster the powerful coherence of shared understanding and shared commitment.

The Condition of Meetings

'Clearly, the only sensible way to do this is to use a pemory widget.'
'We can't use a pemory widget. They cost too much!'
'No, they don't.'
'Yes, they do.'
'Not if you buy them in quantity.'
'We don't need a large quantity.'
'We would if we ever made a decision around here.'
'Besides, they're not on the list of approved widgets yet.'
'Nobody pays attention to that list anyway.'
'Yes, they do.'
'No, they don't.'

Most people complain about meetings. While most managers spend well over half their working time in formal meetings of one sort or another, the complaints 'too many meetings' or 'ineffective meetings' are high in most corporate surveys. (That fact alone illuminates pervasive, chronic organizational pain.)

There are telltale signs of fragmentation brewing under the surface of project meetings. In any given project meeting, one or more participants may:

- continuously whisper or make side comments to each other;
- interrupt each other frequently;

- make points unrelated to either the agenda or the previous point;
- speak unclearly, use jargon, or ramble aimlessly;
- sit in sullen silence without participating at all;
- make the same point over and over;
- harbor secret agendas;
- raise issues that have been discussed and resolved in the past, as if they were still open;
- get defensive if someone disagrees with them or criticizes a point they made;
- act aggressively, arguing and debating every point;
- remain silent even if they know the real issue is not being discussed, or is not even discussible;
- pretend to accept a group decision without actually intending to comply with or implement it.

Sound familiar? There is a tendency to regard these behaviors as normal, or as 'just the way people are.' Most of us have learned to make allowances for these behaviors, or even justify them (e.g., 'employees need to let off steam with each other'). Part of the condition of fragmentation is believing that painful, ineffective meetings are natural and inevitable.

Sometimes the early-on meetings in a wicked problem project go just fine – everyone is on board and committed, spirits are high, egos subdued, and collaboration is strong. But as things go along, new stakeholders are drawn into the project, and social complexity increases. As major milestones approach, problem wickedness reveals itself . . . stress increases, and stress – like sandpaper on old paint, like driving rain on loose soil – exposes what was under the surface. Deeper emotions are activated, and they leak out, especially under the pressures of looming deadlines and tight budgets. When egos are threatened, the reptilian brain responds with basic fight/flight instincts. The project turns into a battlefield.

It is tempting to suspect that project meetings look the way they do because people are ill bred or under-trained. One solution is training – courses, seminars, and workshops that impart new knowledge to employees about better ways to act and interact. As an extension of the socialization process, this approach has its place in the human resources toolkit. But the modern knowledge worker does not need additional training in how to behave – he and she need better tools for dealing with social complexity, for managing the nonlinear flow of opportunity-driven cognition, for constructing coherent views of the mess created by fragmentation and information overload.

Collaborative Display

In his wonderful book *No More Teams: Mastering the Dynamics of Creative Collaboration*, Michael Schrage introduces a most important new distinction in collaborative technology: *shared space*. 'Shared space literally adds a new dimension to conversation, a dimension embracing symbolic representation, manipulation, and memory. . . . It takes shared space to create shared understandings' (Schrage, 1995, p. 94).

In the years since Schrage wrote those lines, the terms 'shared space' and 'shared display' have entered mainstream vocabulary. (Not just in collaborative technology – on some airlines the pre-takeoff announcement includes the injunction to 'Remember that the over-head compartment is shared space – please position your stowed items to use that space as efficiently as possible.') Shared space generally refers to asynchronous situations, such as putting a document on a file server, whereas 'shared display' is used for synchronous situations, namely, the traditional meeting.[2]

In any case, a minimum requirement for any shared medium is that the participants are interacting with it. You may have a really big, brilliant computer screen, but if the people in the meeting are not looking at it, then it is not a shared display (see Figure 2.1).

Figure 2.1   Shared display with a computer and display projector

What makes the concept of shared display particularly powerful at this point in history is that the key enabler, projecting a computer screen on a meeting room wall, is becoming commonplace. Most of the time, this display is just for presentations. When the presentation ends and the discussion starts, you might as well turn off the computer, because everyone takes it for granted that the computer has nothing to offer once people start talking to one another.

Using the computer to create a 'shared display,' however, adds a new dimension to groupwork, involving the participants in interacting with appropriate representations through software projected on a wall or a projection screen. (The best software for dialogue mapping is Compendium – see Appendix for further information.)

This leads to another important distinction: if the group is simply passively observing the display, then it does not truly qualify as 'shared display.' A crowd sitting in a movie theater is sharing an experience, but the display does not respond to their actions, so it is not a shared display. Similarly, a PowerPoint® presentation is only shared display if the presenter is actively changing and expanding each slide based on 'audience' input.

Since shared display is fundamentally interactive and collaborative, we will use the more precise term 'collaborative display.'

The collaborative display functions as a dynamic 'boundary object'[3] that mediates the flow of conversation in the meeting. As abstract concepts are reified in the display they become stable building blocks in the conversation, encouraging conversational moves that refer to and build on previous moves. The display is used by the facilitator to register the contributions of each person in the group, to welcome a diversity of perspectives, and to craft a representation that encompasses the full diversity of concerns and creative thinking in the group.

The role of the dialogue mapper is crucial in making collaborate display effective. It is much more than just being a stenographer or scribe for the group. Ultimately, the dialogue mapper is responsible for being the bridge between the group and the collaborative display, which involves:

- actively *listening* to the conversation;
- *summarizing* the conversational moves in the collaborative display using the IBIS argumentation structure;
- incrementally *validating* the map so that group members accept and own the map as a faithful representation of their thinking.

Beyond the mechanics there is something transcendental that happens when facilitating with a collaborative display is really working. It is beyond mechanical skill or cognitive understanding. There is a gestalt – a relationship among the people in the group and the display and the conversation – that is itself phenomenal. Literally, a phenomenon. Like 'being in the zone' in sports or excellence in the performance arts (and dialogue mapping is a performance art!), there is a moment when everything comes together and becomes a single flow – a dance. At this point you go beyond understanding collaborative display – you grok[4] it.

I've had the privilege of experiencing this moment with groups on several occasions. The meeting has been grinding along as the participants play their roles: the experts, the leaders, the quiet ones, the underlings, the ones reading email on their Blackberries. The problem is messy and complex. The dialogue mapper is capturing conversational moves in the map, but the participants are directing their comments to each other and paying little heed to the map. There's an undercurrent of debate and points being scored.

But then something happens. The dialogue mapper has asked for clarification of a point in the map. Suddenly, the group is looking at the display, and as they study the map they see the individual comments, but they also see The Bigger Picture, the higher order, of the complex subject they are trying to discuss. They remember why they came to the meeting, and they start trusting that they aren't as lost and confused as they thought they were.

And the group starts to interact with the display. It becomes their display. They point at it and comment on it, ask for changes, and direct their comments to each other *and into the display*. Instead of trudging behind the conversation, trying to keep up, the dialogue mapper and the shared display enter the sense-making dance.

This is what collaborative display is really about. It's the magical phenomenon of socially shared cognition. It goes beyond anything that most people have ever experienced in a corporate setting. Collaborative display is a fundamental breakthrough in the art and craft of collaboration. It provides a medium, a tool, a vehicle, a container for collective sense making. It transcends technology or individual achievement – it is made of the same stuff as a choir singing divinely or a volleyball team in perfect synch. It's about this breakthrough in collaboration science that is emerging because its time has come. This breakthrough is really what this book is all about (Box 2.1 contains an example).

Box 2.1 Dialogue mapping field report

One dialogue mapping practitioner, Jeffrey, reports that he used dialogue mapping for a very difficult negotiation between three labor unions.

There was a bitter division among the three union groups, and as the day wore on the tension got higher and higher. Some people started to make personal remarks about others, and it seemed likely that a fistfight was going to break out soon. The convener of the meeting leaned over to Jeffrey and suggested it was time for a break. Jeffrey, in a bold move, quietly said, 'Just give me five more minutes.' Jeffrey then stopped the discussion, got everyone to look at the map, and, pointing to one part of the map, asked, 'Can we agree about this one point?'

Several people immediately responded, 'No!'

'Then, can we agree upon this issue – and this "wish" – as you shared them with me, almost universally, during our one-on-one interviews.'

Everyone in the group agreed that the question Jeffrey was pointing to was their irreconcilable difference. 'Then what we need to do *today* is agree that this is the real issue we're dealing with. No more smoke screens. Then, given what you've shared with me and with each other during the course of the day, everything you see on the wall and on the map, we need to decide and agree upon one of these three options . . . or go home having accomplished nothing. My home is really too far away for me to "come back tomorrow," so my choice – and my challenge to you – is to resolve this right now, right here.'

There was a silence for a moment, and then two of the labor leaders changed their seats to sit next to the third – no prompting, no remarks. They spoke for a moment together and then asked Jeffrey a question about an idea posted with one of the options. Jeff answered their question, with the concurrence of the meeting's convener, and they returned to their seats. There was silence for a moment, and then . . . a decision. The 'loudest' of the leaders spoke for the three of them. 'We agree that we have "named our pain" – as you put it – and agree that we have addressed all of our concerns and our ideas. Option Three looks to be the best solution for all of us. If management will support it then you have our support, and our thanks. We've been arguing over these issues for almost 20 years – it's time to resolve them.' It was a breakthrough.

By getting the group to focus on the logic of the issue in the map, Jeffrey was able to get all three groups to agree to *something* for a moment, and that moment broke the spell of intransigent warfare that had dominated the interaction for the whole day.

Why There's so much Repetition in Meetings

Try this experiment. Find a colleague, and challenge them to three games of Noughts and Crosses (in the USA, Tic-Tac-Toe) in three minutes. But . . . there's a twist: You're not allowed to write anything down. You just talk through the game . . . just as professionals conduct project meetings. Playing Noughts and Crosses without writing anything down is chal-  lenging, but not impossible, and most of us can manage to complete at least two games successfully within the time allotted. Now, do the exercise again, this time on a 4 × 4 grid. This, you will discover, is virtually impossible.

The problem is that humans have a very limited short-term memory. This was shown by Bell Labs researchers 50 years ago, who demonstrated that humans are pretty good at remembering sets of seven digits, and designed the telephone numbering system accordingly. Classic Noughts and Crosses requires keeping track of nine values, which is within the average range of human capacity. However, playing 4 × 4 Noughts and Crosses means following 16 different values, which, for most of us, overflows our short-term memory.

This basic human limitation is one reason why meetings are often so inefficient. Because people have limited memories, and because we are often unsure of whether or not our ideas have been heard and are being taken seriously, we often spend the bulk of a meeting repeating the same thing over and over again. This repetition cycle makes meetings inefficient, if not painful.

Recording ideas in a collaborative display while they are being proposed is one way to address this problem. Simply writing down the idea so that everyone can see it is an instant, visual way of saying, 'I heard you, and I'm taking you seriously.'

Mechanics of Collaborative Display

Collaborative display combines three familiar elements – software, method, and facilitation – in a new way that seems to make it 'go' (also see Conklin, Selvin, Buckingham Shum and Sierhuis, 2003 for more detail). More precisely, these components (Figure 2.2) are called:

1 *display* – some shared display medium such as a computer projector, flipchart paper, or a whiteboard;
2 *notation* – a grammar or method that provides the 'rules' for how the content is to be structured in the display medium;
3 *mapping* – a person skilled in capturing group interactions in the display according to the notation (also referred to as the 'facilitator' or 'technographer' (DeKoven, 1990)).

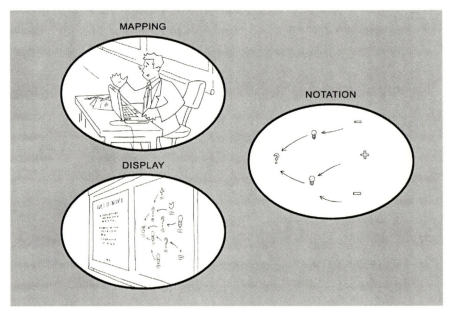

Figure 2.2 The three elements of dialogue mapping in action

Dialogue mapping is a specific form of collaborative display in which the notation used is the IBIS argumentation grammar. There are other forms of collaborative display, using other grammars. Dynamic facilitation (Rough, 1997), for example, is a low-tech variation on dialogue mapping, in which a facilitator captures comments from the group on four flipchart pages, labeled 'problem statements,' 'solutions,' 'concerns,' and 'data.' These categories, then, are the 'grammar' of dynamic facilitation, and flipchart pages taped to the wall are the display.

Each of three elements – display, notation, and mapping – is essential to the mechanics of building shared understanding (Figure 2.3).

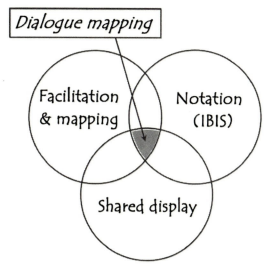

Figure 2.3 The three ingredients that make up collaborative display

You must have someone facilitating and mapping the conversation. This requires linguistic abilities and group interaction skills, and cannot be automated or done in a mechanical way.

If someone is recording participants' contributions but there is no shared display, then the group cannot see and interact with the model. This is why traditional meeting minutes, no matter how accurate and complete, do not add to a meeting's coherence.

And if someone is facilitating and mapping in a shared display, but there is no structural notation for the contents of the display, then there is a limit to how much material can be included before it becomes a big jumble of stuff.

Research in collaborative display has found that the biggest challenge is finding a notation with the right level of complexity and expressive power (Kirschner *et al.*, 2003). If the notation is too simple (e.g., a list, or random boxes and arrows scattered around), it will run out of gas long before the full complexity of the group's thinking is reflected in it. If the notation is too complicated, it will be too hard for the group to use it transparently – they'll have to focus too much energy on learning the grammar and building the representation.

For example, the limitation that facilitators frequently run into when making a simple list of comments is that the notation is not rich enough. Someone will get up and make a list on a flipchart, or sketch a picture or diagram, and for a few minutes that shared display will serve the group very well. People will gesture toward the display as they speak, referring to elements of it, or get up and add or change something in it. The shared display is working: it's boosting shared understanding. But at some point, if the problem has any wickedness at all, two people will disagree about what should be in the display . . . about whether an activity should be part of the project, say, or whether the database should be in the main module or a separate module. As soon as there is disagreement about the model, the tendency is to ignore the disagreement or stop using the shared display, because the notation can't deal with conflict or disagreement.

This is where IBIS shines as a shared display notation. IBIS begs for disagreement! IBIS eats disagreement and debate for breakfast! IBIS says, 'You don't think that's a good idea? Great! Give me an argument against it and I'll put it in the display. Or, give me a different idea . . . I'll capture that. Think we're on the wrong issue? Terrific – let's get a new question up in the display!' The IBIS argumentation scheme was designed for problem solving, decision making, and design conversations. IBIS is what makes dialogue mapping a good match for creative situations. It allows for and embraces disagreement about what the problem is and how to solve it, and helps the group see the structure of their analysis in an intuitive way. Most importantly, it continues to add coherence as a group's process plunges into the roller coaster ride of opportunity-driven problem solving.

Like welding, upholstery, or glass blowing, dialogue mapping is a *craft skill*, not a cut-and-dried technique. Therefore, it takes considerable practice to do well. The good news is that, even done poorly, collaborative display can add value to group reflection and enhance communication and shared understanding. By drawing the group's attention to the collaborative display, the dialogue mapper focuses group energy on what everyone has in common (the display) and defocuses the differences among the participants.

A final note on the mechanics of dialogue mapping: experienced facilitators sometimes find they need to *unlearn* some of their group interaction skills to make effective use of the shared display. Dialogue mapping does not have a 'process' in the same way many other facilitation approaches do – there is no sequence of activities, no prescribed starting point or ending point. It is not even necessary to start the map with a question. Typically, a group naturally starts with several related questions of the sort 'What should we do about X?' and 'How should we do Y?' Along the way, questions of fact ('What is the case about X?') and meaning ('What does X mean?') emerge and are addressed. A complete map usually includes exploration of the questions 'Who are the stakeholders?' and 'What are the decision criteria?' But all these organizing questions come from the group, in their own time.

Indeed, one feature of collaborative display, and especially of dialogue mapping, is that it can work with groups exactly the way they are. Participants are not asked to change their behavior or to march in step to a predefined process. To be sure, the mapping process affects the group's behavior, but it does not restrict or regiment the content or flow of the dialog.

Features of Collaborative Display

Let's review what collaborative display has to offer to project teams. Teased apart, there are seven distinct features of collaborative display:

1 The display acts as a *memory system* that augments the group's collective short-term memory (STM). It is common to see groups start to repeat themselves, or get lost and muddled when they lack a shared display of their conversation – it usually takes around 20 minutes to an hour. The collaborative display helps reduce the use of 'truth by repetition.' If someone repeats a point they've made earlier, the dialogue mapper simply points to their comment, already in the display, and asks 'Is this what you mean?' The speaker quickly gets the point that repeating a point for emphasis has lost its teeth. It has become more embarrassing than persuasive.

   Moreover, the memory-augmenting display really helps when the problem is wicked. Wickedness means the group is dealing with hundreds of issues, chunks of knowledge, points of view, etc. and they don't all make sense together. As the Tic-Tac-Toe example illustrates, it is very hard to hold a pile of disconnected pieces of information in the head. Groups dealing with really complex problems come to trust that most of the relevant bits are in the display, even if they don't know how it all fits together yet.

2 The memory system aspect of collaborative display also contributes to the long-term memory (LTM) of the group, also known as 'group memory.' Currently, groups use meeting minutes for this, but there are many well-documented problems with the traditional meeting minutes document. It is incomplete, it represents one person's interpretation of what happened and what was said, if it contains errors they don't get fixed until after the meeting (and perhaps never), and usually it arrives after the energy of the meeting has died out (DeKoven, 1990). Moreover, meeting minutes documents don't constitute an effective group memory in terms of retrieval and lookup. Using a collaborative display, however, the 'minutes' literally become the collaborative product of the meeting. The work of the group becomes collectively crafting the map in the collaborative display, which can contain everything that was said, validated on the spot, and available in hard copy during and immediately after the meeting. And IBIS organizes the cumulative group memory in terms of *questions*, so the information is structured by the issues.

3 Indeed, the whole purpose and mood of meetings changes when a collaborative display is used. As DeKoven points out, 'communication becomes production' (DeKoven, 1990, p. 109). People change their focus from 'meeting together to producing together.' The focus on using every meeting to produce a collaborative product (the dialogue map) has a profound impact on the waste-of-time condition of most meetings, because everyone can see visible progress as the meeting proceeds. People are less likely to come to the meeting passive and resigned if they anticipate that production is automatically a part of the meeting process. We are not just sitting around talking, we are creating something

together. I've seen far fewer bored-looking people in meetings that used a collaborative display than traditional 'just talking' meetings.

4   Another significant feature of dialogue mapping collaborative display is the flexibility of IBIS as the notation of the display. While other problem structuring methods involve collaborative display, and thus have the features listed above, IBIS introduces a very distinct element: every comment is captured according to a rhetorical notation . . . Questions, Ideas, Pros, and Cons. The use of an argumentation scheme means that fluency in the notation takes a bit more practice, but it offers an amazing benefit. When the conversation gets really confused, and the interaction temperature is beginning to rise, the IBIS map can elegantly expose that the debate is really over two different issues, for example, or is simply a tension between two good ideas. IBIS promotes an energetic shift from trying to 'be right' or 'win the argument' to making the strongest possible logical case for a proposal. Done well it exposes an elegant order underlying chaotic and contentious discussions. This emergent order enhances the group's intellectual integrity, allows the group to learn together much faster, and encourages out-of-the-box thinking.

5   Shared display provides a single focus for the group's attention. By 'putting something in the middle' (Palus and Drath, 2001), the energy shifts, as when a group is discussing a diagram on the wall or a sketch on the table. The display orients the conversation. Since everyone is paying attention to the display, everyone is oriented in the same direction, looking at the same map. This creates a mood of collaboration, however subtly, even if the participants are deeply divided over the content of the discussion.

6   The collaborative display is a powerful *listening tool*. Like the talking stick, the display makes it very clear who has the floor at

any moment – the person the dialogue mapper is listening to and capturing. Having and using this powerful listening tool *makes the dialogue mapper the designated listener for the group*. As a result, each person who speaks experiences being heard. Even if no one else is listening, the dialogue mapper is honoring the group and each person in it by listening, capturing, and validating their point of view. This in itself is a profound breakthrough in corporate culture.

Since everyone is being honored with the same quality of listening, dialogue mapping levels the playing field, creating a very democratic environment in the group. The boss still has final authority in the decision, but the process of exploring the issues is open and rational, and group consensus is shaped more by effective case making and clear thinking than by rhetoric or title.

7 The collaborative display acts as a sort of 'mirror' in which the group can see itself more clearly, especially its behavior. Disruptive behavior patterns show up rather obviously. If a participant goes off topic with a comment, the dialogue mapper can work with him or her to find out how to capture the comment either as a new question or as a node linked to an existing part of the map; either way, the topic shift shows up clearly in the geometry of the map. If a participant challenges the whole frame of the meeting (e.g., 'Why are we talking about this? This isn't the real issue?') the dialogue mapper can capture that comment in a clear way – a 'left-hand move' – that captures the participant's concern and any discussion about it without undermining the rest of the meeting's discussion. If someone asks a closed question (e.g., 'Should we abandon that product line?'), the yes/no options in the map reflect the limiting frame of the question. Thus the dialogue map allows the group to clearly see the conversational patterns it uses, and supports organically upgrading those patterns into more

productive ones. (Figure 2.4 shows an IBIS map for what we have discussed in this section.)

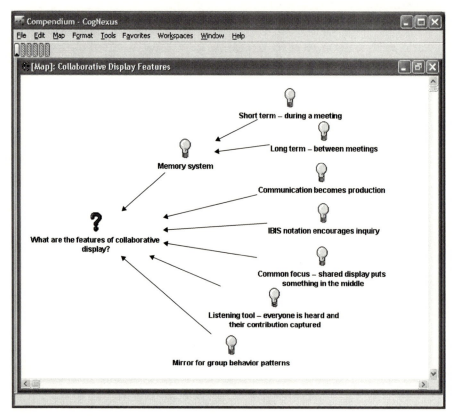

Figure 2.4 IBIS map of this section of the chapter

Beyond the Meeting Room

Collaboration extends beyond conference rooms in both time and space. Groups routinely conduct virtual meetings using teleconferencing and shared desktop systems such as Webex™. Another kind of virtual meeting, using threaded discussion tools, allows discussions to unfold asynchronously, offering the time-shifting convenience of email. Teams no longer need to be collocated in order to work together.

Dialogue mapping supports synchronous meetings with a distributed group very well. In conjunction with a teleconference, the dialogue mapper shares his or her Compendium screen with the group using a web-based shared desktop system – collaborative display on the Internet! Each participant, sitting in front of their computer, can watch as the dialogue mapper captures and maps the comments being made in the phone call. Indeed, some practitioners have reported that such virtual meetings can be *more* productive than face-to-face sessions, evidently because there are fewer distractions.

Admittedly, project work extends beyond meetings to all the activity and conversation that happens *between* meetings. Ultimately we need a *system* to manage the chaotic flow of information, issues, and decisions, and to make it more coherent.

Dialogue mapping is a beginning . . . a first step toward a truly robust and comprehensive issue management system. And such a system must start in meetings, because that's where the social network assembles to make sense of its wicked problem.

Attempts to start with capturing and 'managing knowledge' have a poor track record because knowledge must be treated more as a conversational process than a frozen asset. As currently practiced, knowledge management tools fail to make contact with the issues and decisions that surface and explode in meetings.

We stand at the beginning of a revolutionary endeavor to create humane, ecological, and effective ways of dealing with 'issues' (i.e.

messy, dynamic conversations among diverse stakeholders) across the weeks, months, and years that most projects span. The first step is to counter fragmentation where its impact is the greatest: in meetings. Eventually the day will come when every project meeting results in a dialogue map, and dialogue maps will be living documents that grow and evolve and focus the conversations of the whole project community. At that point we will face a major a technical challenge: how to maintain and organize and retrieve this massive corpus of formal and informal project information. But that's a secondary problem, and not an especially wicked one![5]

First, we have to create the maps that make the meetings work – consistently, meeting by meeting, over time. That will give us the raw material for the next exciting phase of discovery: how to manage, track, maintain, refine, and search a hypertext compendium of project and organizational knowledge. (For a case study of an organization that has over 12 years of experience with this kind of environment, see Conklin, 2003.)

Notes

1. The notion of augmenting human intellect and collaboration capacity has been powerfully advanced and championed by Doug Engelbart (Engelbart, 1963), the inventor of the computer mouse, hypertext, and dozens of other innovations, for which he was given the US National Medal of Technology. Dialogue mapping owes an enormous debt to Engelbart's pioneering work.
2. Schrage used the term 'shared space' for all situations: 'Shared spaces can be divorced from time or space, or both' (p. 95). The computer interface research community generally uses 'shared display' for synchronous

but physically remote situations, in which each party is looking at its own computer screen. The discussion in this chapter applies to both traditional and electronic meetings, but focuses on traditional collocated meeting settings.

3. 'Boundary objects are those objects that both inhabit several communities of practice and satisfy the informational requirements of each of them. Boundary objects are thus both plastic enough to adapt to local needs and constraints of the several parties employing them, yet robust enough to maintain a common identity across sites. They are weakly structured in common use and become strongly structured in individual site use. These objects may be abstract or concrete . . . Such objects have different meanings in different social worlds but their structure is common enough to more than one world to make them recognizable, a means of translation. The creation and management of boundary objects is a key process in developing and maintaining coherence across intersecting communities' (Bowker and Star, 1999, p. 297).

4. 'To understand profoundly through intuition or empathy' (www. dictionary.com).

5. Doug Engelbart and his Bootstrap Institute have been studying that problem for over 40 years, and have a sound program for solving it. See http://www.bootstrap.org/engelbart/index.jsp.

Summary

To briefly summarize the key points of this chapter:

1 Collective intelligence is a natural property of human social groups, but, like the immune system, it can be compromised by a harsh and toxic environment, i.e. the environment created by fragmenting forces such as problem wickedness and social complexity.

2 The 'fuel' for collective intelligence is shared understanding combined with shared commitment.

3 Collaborative display is a practical and robust technique for creating shared understanding and shared commitment.

4 Dialogue mapping is a specific form of collaborative display.

Or, at the risk of oversimplifying, *shared display gives shared understanding*.

3
The Dialogue Mapping Experience

One of the first things we do in our training workshops is to have a demonstration dialogue mapping session. We pick a nice wicked problem like reducing violence in schools or ending world hunger and I facilitate and dialogue map the class's discussion on the topic for 10 or 15 minutes. This lets everyone directly experience what the 'target' is in terms of what the dialogue mapper is doing and what it feels like to be a participant in such a session. It gets us out of conceptualizing about design and into the concrete reality of people trying to talk to each other about a messy but important topic.

This chapter is that demo session for you. OK, sure, it's still like reading about skiing instead of actually *skiing*. For this chapter to work you have to sort of give yourself to it . . . *pretend* you're having the experience of being in a real meeting! Pretend you work for a medium size software company named 'SpinCo' and you care about the company and your job. At the end you can have your *real* company and job back. OK? Here we go . . .

You are barely on time for the meeting. You enter the meeting room with your notebook and pen and some mail to read in case things drag during the meeting. You've been thinking about suggesting a new product idea for the company, but you suspect it won't be easy. There is already a lot of confusion in the marketplace about what business SpinCo is really in, and a new product could make matters worse. Plus there a few people coming to the meeting who are dedicated to their own products, and will probably perceive anything new as competing for scarce investment resources. But, it's not like *their* products are doing so well, and the company definitely needs something to give it focus and momentum. You'd like to get some discussion of your idea, but the last time someone brought up a new product idea there was a lot of resistance to even considering it, and the meeting dragged on without really going anywhere. You could have really used a stack of mail at *that* meeting!

As you settle in your seat you notice someone new at the table, with a notebook computer in front of him. His computer is connected to a display projector. Is there going to be a demo at this meeting?, you wonder. The new guy is sitting next to Beth, who called this meeting. Beth is a good manager – she's got a good head, has some seniority in the company, and knows a lot about technology. Sometimes her meetings get lost in the weeds, and she tends to go on sometimes, but at least when she does she's passionate about what she says. Beth introduces the new guy, Jamie, as a facilitator who will use the computer to help keep the meeting on track. She explains it's an experiment, and she's interested in feedback from the group on how it goes afterward.

Jamie flips on the screen and you see the agenda for the meeting, but it's not in PowerPoint. There are icons with text under them (see Figure 3.1), and arrows connecting the icons together. On the left is a question mark icon labeled 'Agenda?' and connected to it on the right are several light bulb icons with labels like 'Status report from Jim,' 'Sales figures,' and 'Action items.' (Why do the arrows go backward?, you wonder.)

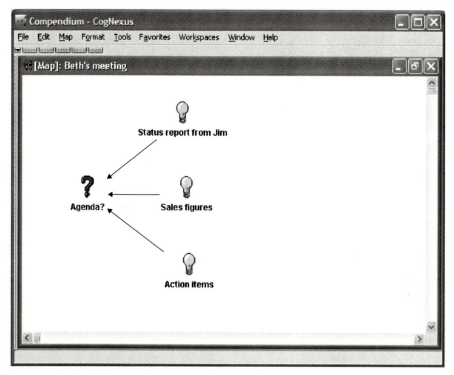

Figure 3.1 Original IBIS agenda map for Beth's meeting

Jamie reads through the diagram, and then asks if there are any other items for the agenda. So far, it's pretty clear what he's doing, although it not clear that the group needs all this technology for this – the agenda is really simple. There is a pause, so you think, What the heck, and you say that you've got a new product idea that you would like to propose informally. You half expect Beth to say that she doesn't

want to discuss new products today, but she is looking at the screen.
Without any pause Jamie says, 'What kind of product?' 'It would be
a service, sort of like our XIT offering,' you say, doubting that Jamie
knows anything about XIT. Without hesitating, Jamie creates a new
light bulb icon and labels it 'New service product idea.' Then he links
it to the 'Agenda?' question. Well, you think . . . at least he's listening (see Figure 3.2).

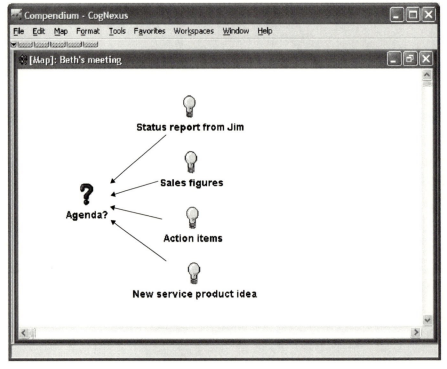

Figure 3.2 A new agenda item is added

You sit up a little more in your chair. OK, you're committed now. You
notice that Burt, the XIT product manager, is looking at the screen,
and you think you can hear him sharpening his knives for a battle.

Burt's good, he really knows his stuff, but he can be pretty argumentative.

Jamie asks if there are any other items for the agenda, but no one else speaks up. You look at the screen and think, 'That's not a big agenda . . . I might just get called on to present this idea.' You open your notebook and start making notes of the key things you want to say.

Jamie calls for the first agenda item, the status report from Jim. At the same time, he creates a new icon on the screen, labels it 'Jim's status report' and then opens up a new blank window. As he's typing he asks Jim, 'What's the name of your project?' Jim replies, 'Deli-quick.' Jamie quickly creates a new Question icon, labels it 'Status of Deli-quick?,' and then stops and looks at Jim (see Figure 3.3). You

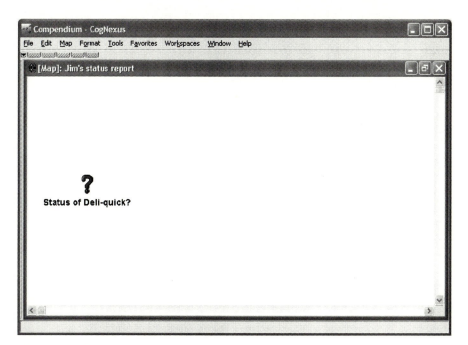

Figure 3.3   Beginning map for Jim's status report

notice that Jamie seems very comfortable with his role. He seems alert and energetic.

Jim says, 'I guess everyone knows that there's been a problem with our ASP, InfoServe. At the beginning of the month they were two weeks behind schedule on our design review, and it was beginning to put our schedule at risk. That's all we needed, another delay.' As Jim speaks, Jamie is typing. An idea icon appears, and the label beneath it taps out 'InfoServe was 2 weeks behind schedule' (see Figure 3.4). Jim goes on, 'So we had a meeting with them on Monday, and they were very aware of the problem, and very apologetic, and they are going to give us a Beta release right away and have the final release by the end of the month.'

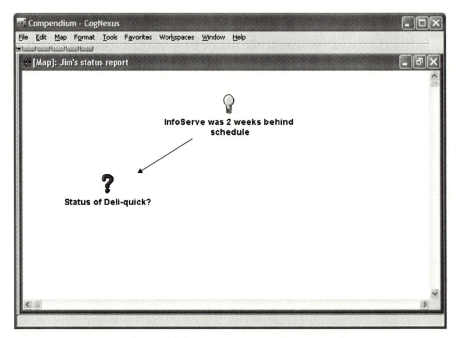

Figure 3.4 A new node is added to Jim's status report map

Jim starts to go on, but Jamie quickly interrupts. 'So, you'll get the Beta release right away' and a new idea icon appears labeled 'Will get Beta release right away.' 'Do you know when you'll get it, Jim?' Jamie asks. Jim responds, 'They said by close of business on Friday.' Jamie deletes the 'right away' and taps in a few letters – the new label says 'Will get Beta release by COB Friday.' Jamie asks 'Is that right?' and Jim nods, saying 'Yeah, and the final release by the end of the month.' As he's typing, Jamie says 'Good. Right. Got it.' and a new idea appears labeled 'Will get final release by end of March' (see Figure 3.5). Jamie glances up at Jim and asks, 'Is there anything you're supposed to do to make that happen?' and Jim shakes his head slowly, 'No, we didn't commit to do anything.' Jamie nods and says 'OK.'

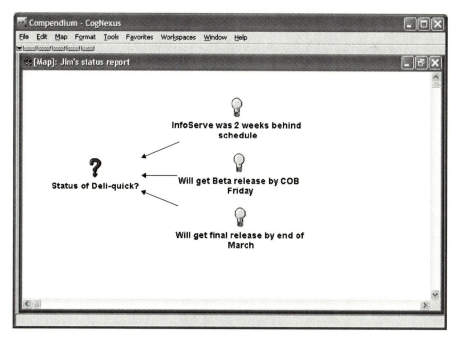

Figure 3.5 A snapshot of Jim's status report map

Jamie seems to be tracking the conversation closely. You wonder if he's been in the ASP business for a long time – he seems to be pretty familiar with it.

As the meeting goes on, Jamie continues to capture the main points that each person is making, sometimes as questions, sometime as light bulbs, all connected together. You notice that even if your mind wanders, you can glance up at the screen and see the flow of the conversation in the diagram. As the map gets bigger, there's a sense of progress. There's also a sense that the group is more focused, everyone seems to be paying attention. Usually by now there would have been a couple of side conversations that distracted the group from the purpose of the meeting.

Your agenda item is next. Just as he has done with the other topics, Jamie creates a new empty map, opens the window, and creates a new Question icon. He pauses and looks at you. 'I'm going to make this an open question, so we can capture the whole conversation, but the intent is to capture your idea as fully as possible, OK?' You nod, and he types 'What new products should we consider?' 'Tell us about it,' he says to you. He seems to be interested, which makes it a little easier to press on.

You glance at your notes. 'This started out from a lunch conversation with Heidi. She was telling me about an incident with one of her SpinFast clients, and it struck me that with SpinFast and some of our other products, we are basically leaving money on the table. These clients are all trying to do some strategic planning around acquiring and rolling out our products, but we have to send them elsewhere for help with the planning process. And by now we've seen enough of it that we're practically experts – we certainly know how *not* to do it!'

As you pause, Jamie says, 'So the new product would be a strategic planning service?'

'That's right,' you say, 'IT system rollout strategic planning.' Jamie starts typing a new light bulb 'IT system rollout strategic planning.'

Jamie says, 'And I heard you say that clients need it and have to go elsewhere, and we're becoming experts at it.' Near the light bulb, Jamie creates two new icons, big green plus signs, and labels them 'Clients are getting it elsewhere' and 'We are experts' (see Figure 3.6). As he is typing you elaborate. 'That's right – this SpinFast client had to hold up the whole rollout because they couldn't find anybody, evidently, to take their organization through the kind of process that worked so well for the Zephyr folks last year.'

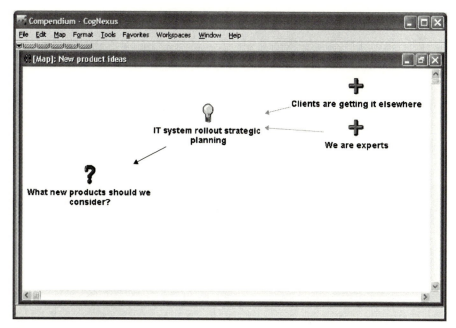

Figure 3.6 A new product idea and two supporting arguments

Jamie has double-clicked on the big green plus icon labeled 'Clients are getting it elsewhere' – opening up a new 'Node contents' window that sort of looks like an email message. In the big part of the window called 'Detail' he has been typing.

'Hang on just a sec,' he says. 'Here's what I've got so far: "Heidi's client couldn't find consultant to do planning process. Zephyr had successful process last year." Is that right? Does that capture it?' (see Figure 3.7).

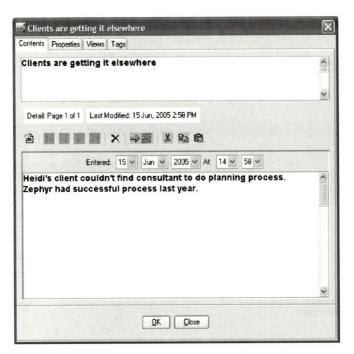

Figure 3.7 Every node can have a detail, like the text of an email

'Yes,' you say, 'Zephyr is a good example of a planning process that ran well. We were there, we watched what their consultants did, and they got a lot of good input and buy-in to the system before it was rolled out.'

'Ohhh, I get it,' Jamie says. He deftly moves the text 'Zephyr had successful process last year' to the detail of the 'We are experts' node, and then types 'and we learned how from watching it.' As he's typing he reads out loud, glancing at the screen, and ends saying 'Is that it?'

'Well,' you say, 'I don't think we're experts. It's just that we've seen it done a lot and we pretty well know how to do it.'

Jamie quickly replaces 'We are experts' with 'We know how.'

'OK?' he says, looking at you.

'Yep, that's it.'

You are about to go on when Burt says, 'I have one small question here,' in that way that means 'That is a dumb idea and I'm gonna show you why.' You have heard his 'small questions' before and you know what is coming.

But before Burt gets any further Jamie quickly says to him, 'Sorry, hang on just a second. I'll be right there.' Then glancing at you as he turns to the screen Jamie says, 'So, here's what I've got so far. I just want to check it.'

Speaking quickly and motioning on the screen (see Figure 3.8) with the cursor, Jamie says, 'The proposal is for a new service that does IT rollout strategic planning, and so far there are two plusses for this

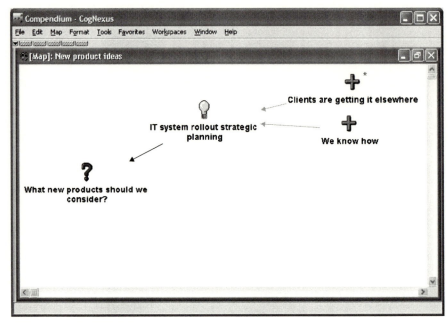

Figure 3.8 A node's 'detail' can be read out directly from the map

idea, one is "Clients are getting it elsewhere" and the other is "We know how".'

'Oh, yes,' Jamie says while opening up the upper green plus labeled 'Clients are getting it elsewhere.' As he types he says, 'And we're leaving money on the table' (see Figure 3.9).

'Right?' he says, glancing at you.

'Right!' you respond. Beth is looking at the screen (see Figure 3.8) and nodding, and so are several others. It's impressive that Jamie has distilled your idea into just a few nodes – it's very clear and, you think, pretty compelling.

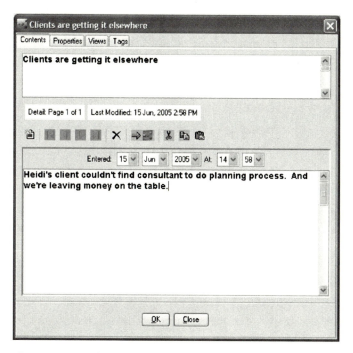

Figure 3.9 Updated detail of first argument

Turning back to Burt, who isn't nodding, Jamie says, 'Sorry. You had a question.'

'Here's my question,' Burt says. 'We started out as a software company, and most of our products are software products. We *know* how to do software really well. We aren't a bunch of consultants. I mean, the whole thing these days is that we're trying to focus, because we've been so scattered. So who is going to do this strategic planning consulting? You??'

He's looking right at you, but before you can respond, Jamie intervenes.

'Let me see if I got that,' he says. On the screen is a new icon, a big red minus sign. 'I captured that as an objection to the idea. "We are a software company",' he says, pointing with the cursor.

Jamie adds, 'I also heard you suggest that we don't have the staff to do that kind of consulting.' He creates another con node and labels it 'Don't have consulting staff.' He links both of the 'con' nodes back to your idea.

'Well, that's true . . . at the moment,' you say to Burt. 'That is the obvious challenge with this idea.'

'So, is there a question, like "How to get consulting staff?" about this proposal?' Jamie asks the room. Both you and Beth respond, 'Yes.' Jamie creates a new question and links it to the idea (see Figure 3.10).

'It's almost three, and I've got another meeting,' Beth announces. 'This has been a really productive meeting. I'd like to thank Jamie for coming, and I'd like to get any input that anybody has. There's a possibility SpinCo will start using this process in our meetings. Just send me an email with your thoughts.'

Turning to you, Beth says, 'I like your idea. I think you're right that we're leaving money on the table. But if I'm going to take it to upper management I'm going to need more clarity about how it would impact our staffing. Let's think about how we might get into that business, and discuss our staffing options at our meeting next week. OK?' As you nod she says, 'Thanks, everybody.'

Jamie is busily typing. As you stand up he says to you, 'I'll send you this map in email, including the action item' (see Figure 3.11).

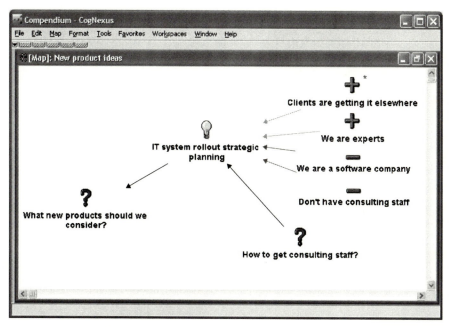

Figure 3.10 Final new products discussion map

'Thanks,' you say. 'I think you really helped us here today. And I've sure got my work cut out for me!' Standing up and collecting your things, you notice you never touched your mail.

Three important points about this example. First, this scenario is simple so that it can be understood without a lot of technical background or hard thinking. It would be a mistake to conclude that dialogue mapping is only for simple problems. Maps can get very large and complex, with hundreds of nodes in a map and many levels of maps nested in other maps. The process and software has been used on some very large projects.

For example, I used dialogue mapping with a cross-functional group of 25 people at a large California electric utility to develop an envi-

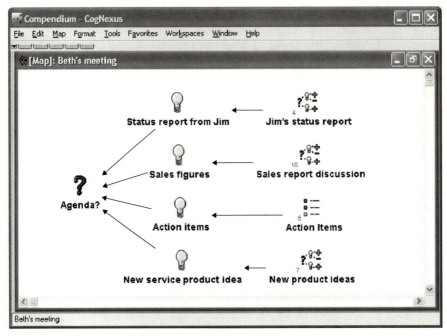

Figure 3.11   Final snapshot of meeting overview map

ronmental 'scorecard' system for the corporation. There were four plenary meetings, spaced about a month apart, and dozens of small group meetings. All meetings were mapped, and the structure of the scorecard was mapped as well. By the end of the process there were dozens of maps, many with upwards of 100 nodes and links in them. In another example, Bell Atlantic used the system for their Y2K contingency planning. A cross-functional team of eight met several times a week for a four-month period leading up to 1 January, 2000. All meetings were mapped. They constructed a system of hundreds of maps based on a limited palate of templates. Many of the maps are very large and include both qualitative and quantitative data about their systems. In short, large or extended projects produce large maps – managing this goldmine of informal knowledge is an advanced dialogue mapping skill.

This story also illustrates an attitude, a 'way of being,' that Jamie holds as the dialogue mapper in the story, an attitude that is critical to the success of dialogue mapping: Jamie is not a passive scribe; he is not trying to run along behind the participants and transcribe their conversation; he isn't quiet – he talks and even interrupts sometimes; he is an active – you might even say passionate – presence in the room.

What Jamie is passionate about is *listening*. He's passionate about making sure that each person has been actively and accurately heard. He doesn't have any agenda or stake in the content of the meeting – his only agenda is helping the group build a compelling map of their conversation.

Part II

4
IBIS: A Tool for All Reasons

*I*f you can tell me why you say that plan A is great, and I understand your judgements, you have succeeded in objectifying your
space of judgement to me. And although I might not share your
judgement and might not be convinced, I understand you now.

Horst Rittel[1]

In Chapter 2 we saw that dialogue mapping is comprised of (1) a collaborative display, (2) the IBIS notation, and (3) a dialogue mapper
who is actively listening to and capturing the moves in the conversation. We are going to develop all those skills as we go along, starting
here with IBIS, because the notation is easy to learn and can be very
useful even if you never facilitate meetings. IBIS takes the way most
of us think about problems and encodes it in an intuitive framework
that exposes the practical elements of problem solving quite clearly.

IBIS stands for issue-based information system. It is a argumentation scheme that was developed in the 1960s and 70s as a way to
support coordination and planning of political decision processes
(Kunz and Rittel, 1970; Rittel, 1972b; Rittel & Noble, 1989). For
more on the history of IBIS and similar 'argumentation systems,' see
Kirschner *et al.*, 2003.

Because IBIS is simple and intuitive, we'll use examples as the
primary teaching method. We'll start off with a brief introduction to

IBIS, then use a simple example to describe the basic elements of the notation. From there, we'll intersperse more detailed observations about IBIS with examples that reveal patterns of conversation. This will deepen your understanding of IBIS, conversational patterns, and how the two relate to each other.

Jumping In

Let's imagine that you are a member of a school board faced with a budget crunch, and you have been presented with the map in Figure 4.1. An initial question on the left is connected to three 'light bulbs' which connect on to more icons.[2]

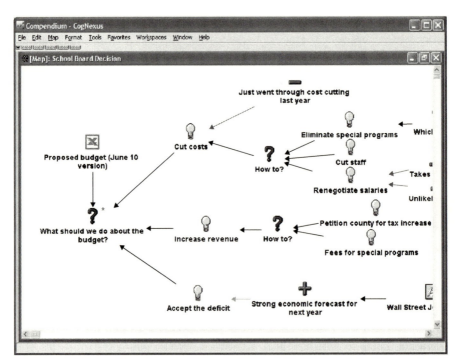

Figure 4.1 A sample dialogue map

Note that the elements of IBIS – Questions, Ideas, Pros and Cons – are relatively familiar and intuitive. You can probably 'read' the map without difficulty. Remember this when you are showing an IBIS map to a new group – they will be happy if you walk them through the *content* of the map, but they won't need much explanation about the notation.

As a dialogue mapper your role is to listen to someone and 'translate' his or her comments into IBIS notation. Let's examine the notation a little deeper.

Maps generally start with Questions, like 'What should we do about the budget?' Questions state a topic or problem to be explored and answered, and end with a question mark. Note that 'The budget issue' is not a Question. Neither is 'We have to decide how to raise the funds.' Whether you are using software or handwriting on a whiteboard, the form of the question is often some variation of 'What should we do about X?'

Dialogue mapping involves the wonderful art of powerful questions, creative and empowering questions, open questions, questions that lead to deep inquiry. Key also is learning to discern hidden questions in a conversation. We'll explore those issues later on in Part III. The basics are marvelously simple: IBIS Questions ask questions.

The response to a Question is an Idea, a possible answer or solution for the Question. Ideas respond to one and only one Question. In the budget map, the main Ideas are 'Cut costs,' 'Increase revenue,' and 'Accept the deficit.' Ideas are neutral. 'Hold a bake sale' is a valid Idea as far as IBIS is concerned. The only requirement for an Idea is that it must be a possible resolution for its Question; in the school board example, 'Eat more fruit' is not a valid Idea on the root Question.

➕ and ▬ The place for rationale, opinion, facts, data, rhetoric, etc. is in the Pros and Cons of IBIS, generically known as Arguments. In the school board map 'Good economic forecast for next year' is a Pro for the Idea 'Accept the deficit.'

A Decision is not really a separate element in IBIS (although the Compendium software has an icon for it) – a Decision is simply *one of the Ideas* on a Question marked as the answer/solution/ decision for that Question. On some Questions there may be several Ideas as the solution.

Questions are the heart and soul of IBIS, because *anything* in the map – a Question, an Idea, a Pro, a Con – can be questioned. Note the secondary Questions 'How to?' in the school board map, and note that each new Question can lead to new Ideas and Pros and Cons. Maps tend to grow from left to right like a tree lying on its side, starting with a 'root' Question, and ending when the group feels done.

IBIS is a very powerful notation,[3] but it's important not to let IBIS take over the mapping process. The map is meant to be primarily a coherent display and record of *what people said* in a conversation. It's not a logic diagram or a decision tree, although it has some of the benefits of those systems. The art of dialogue mapping is to bring just enough logic and notational consistency to the map that it can grow and evolve naturally and organically. If the dialogue mapper is fluent in IBIS and proficient at the 'collaborative display dance' this balance of logic and conversation just flows.

Mission Statement

The president of your corporation, aware of your prowess at consensus building and your fine track record of performance, calls you into his office. 'Tiger' (for some reason, he calls you 'Tiger'), 'I want you to head up a self-directed work team and develop a mission statement for the company.' You learn that four people have been assigned to the team: Joe, Sue, Tom, and Greg, each from different departments. Due to your prowess at facilitation and consensus building, you try to say as little as possible in the first team meeting, allowing the group to self-generate. The following conversation ensues:

You: The President has tasked us with generating a mission statement for the company. It's essential that we get cross-departmental input, so I'd like to hear from everybody.

Joe: Let's make it simple, something like, 'Legendary service.'

Sue: That's way too vague. What about, 'We provide the best product at the best price, and we're committed to providing outstanding service.'

Tom: The main thing is that our computers have the best performance, so we should focus on that.

Joe: ZipCo's computers have superior performance to ours.

You: Shouldn't we say something about our concern for our employees?

Sue: Yeah, and how about the fact that we are committed to being a green corporation, and contributing to society?

Joe: I still like, 'Legendary service.' It's simple. Why do we want it to be complex? No one will remember it.

You: Let's get everyone's input. What about you, Greg?

Greg: Well, I guess I don't understand what the purpose of the mission statement is. We're not talking about a position statement, that's marketing. I think the mission statement should have the employees be excited about the company they are working for.

Joe: If you want to do that, just increase everyone's salaries. Or at least give people better titles. People have been clamoring for that, and it doesn't even cost us anything.

Not normally given to perspiring, you feel a trickle slide down your forehead. This is not going well and likely to get worse. What initially seemed like a career-making opportunity is beginning to look like political suicide. You recall reading something recently about fragmentation and social complexity, and it occurs to you that this project has fragmentation written all over it. You go back to your office and resolve to get enough dialogue mapping under your belt to try it out at the next team meeting.

Let's use the mission statement conversation to take a deeper cut at the IBIS elements, and how to translate from the way people talk into IBIS notation.

You: The President has tasked us with generating a mission statement for the company. It's essential that we get cross-departmental input, so I'd like to hear from everybody.

What is the gist of this statement? You are asking the group to try to come up with a mission statement. In IBIS, you have asked a Question, without stating it as such, and in the map it would be captured something like this:[4]

What should our mission statement be?

The first response is:

Joe: Let's make it simple, something like, 'Legendary service.'

In IBIS, any answer to a Question is called an 'Idea,' and would be captured:

Legendary service

Joe offered some supporting rationale with his suggestion, which in IBIS is reflected in a supporting Argument to the Idea, 'Simple.' Thus Joe's response would be expressed in IBIS as:

Legendary service   Simple

The next response is:

Sue: That's way too vague. What about, 'We provide the best product at the best price, and we're committed to providing outstanding service.'

The first thing Sue does is object to Joe's Idea. In IBIS, this is an objecting Argument, or simply a 'Con':

Too vague

And Sue goes on to immediately offer her own Idea (which is a very common conversational move):

We provide the best product at
the best price and we are
committed to outstanding
service

Alternately, we might paraphrase Sue's suggestion – with her approval – and capture it simply as:

At this point our dialogue map would look like Figure 4.2.

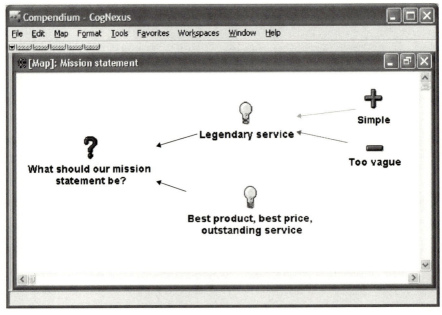

Figure 4.2 Early on in the meeting, a very simple IBIS map

Notice that the arrows point to the left. This is because by convention the maps build from left to right, usually starting with Questions, and the arrows show the direction of the relationship between two nodes, not the order in which they were created. Thus, Ideas *respond to* Questions – the arrow means 'responds to.' Similarly, Pros *support* an Idea and are drawn as an arrow from the Pro to the Idea; and Cons *object to* an Idea and are drawn as an arrow from the Con to the Idea.

Questions, Ideas, Pros and Cons, connected with arrows. There, now you know IBIS! (We'll return to this example shortly.)

Dialogue Mapping without a Computer

There are many benefits to using a computer for dialogue mapping: there is no limit to the size of the maps, it is easy to rearrange maps, you can 'chunk' a set of nodes and links into another map, and at the end of the meeting you can push a button and print copies of the maps for everyone.

However, there are times when it is inconvenient to set up a computer, projector, and screen. In those cases you can dialogue map on any medium that you can write on, using a manual version of the IBIS notation. Called 'Graph IBIS,' this notation lets any flipchart page or whiteboard become a collaborative display. In fact, in the dialogue mapping workshops all the practice exercises are done using Graph IBIS, because it is always useful to have a low-tech backup medium for doing dialogue mapping. Starting with Graph IBIS also lets workshop students jump right into creating IBIS maps without having to learn new software.

The rules of Graph IBIS notation are:

- Questions always have a question mark at the end.
- Ideas link back to Questions.

- Pros and Cons are indicated by '+' and '−' on their link lines.

Figure 4.3 shows the Graph IBIS version of this first part of the meeting (compare to computer map in Figure 4.5, p. 103).

Figure 4.3   Graph IBIS notation of the mission statement issue

Note that in Graph IBIS we don't use icons, just writing and arrows – it just takes too long to sketch the light bulbs and it doesn't add to understanding. Questions always have '?' at the end, Arguments always have '+' or '−' on their links, and everything else is an Idea. Although it is not necessary, I encourage workshop students to put the arrowheads on the link lines, so that it is easier to transition to the software (which requires them). Also, I have found that using 'sentence case' works best – first word capitalized, everything else lower case. It is the easiest to read in large maps, and when transcribed into the software it makes the printouts look much more professional.

Elements of Conversational Structure

IBIS works because it has three essential properties: It is simple, it is intuitive, and it is powerful. The simplicity of IBIS is evident: What could be simpler than questions and answers? What could be more intuitive than pros and cons? This is everyday conversational stuff. You are already a master of IBIS – you use its elements all the time, every day.

It is also intuitive enough that it needs no introduction in a facilitated session; groups comprehend what is happening in the map without an explanation of the IBIS elements.

But knowing the rules of poker doesn't make you a good poker player. The trick to using IBIS as a facilitation notation is fluency – being aware of the pattern of Questions, Ideas, Pros, and Cons as they emerge in everyday speaking style. Seeing the 'deep structure' of a conversation on the fly takes practice, even though the notation is simple and intuitive. This book will provide the basics, but fluency can only come with practice.

The power of IBIS to help create coherence and shared understanding is because it works with virtually *any* design or planning conversation. Just as Niels Bohr revolutionized the understanding of physical matter with his triad model of the atom (proton, neutron, electron), all statements can be understood as built up from the IBIS building blocks (see Figure 4.4). The great advantage of IBIS over other similar modeling notations is that any issue deliberation can be expressed in these elements. I have never run into an interaction that could not be expressed in Questions, Ideas, Pros, and Cons! (Notes, for neutral information, and references, for links to reference documents, are expedient additional elements, but are not essential.) Let's examine the IBIS elements in more detail and explore how to assemble them into the atoms and molecules of conversational structure.

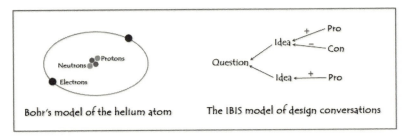

Bohr's model of the helium atom   The IBIS model of design conversations

Figure 4.4 Two triad models that, although very simple, have enormous power

Most conversations in IBIS start with a root Question. This will generally be something like 'What should our marketing approach be?' or 'How can we increase customer "delight" in our products and services?'

The response to a Question is one or more Ideas that offer possible answers to the Question. You can tell an IBIS Idea just by looking at it – it is a neutral statement describing a person, place, thing, or action:

- Build a new inventory system
- Collect data from our customers
- Java
- Provide a toll-free customer support number
- 42 weeks

Capturing an Idea succinctly can be a challenge. Many people tend to bundle several ideas together or bundle the justification for an idea into the presentation of the idea. For example, 'We should provide a toll-free customer support number because it is more inviting for customers to use.' While this is a common way of speaking, the job of the dialogue mapper is to 'unpack' this statement into the (neutral) Idea ('provide a toll-free customer support number') and its supporting Argument ('more inviting for customers to use').

An Argument is an opinion or piece of evidence that either supports or objects to one or more Ideas. Arguments are the place – indeed, the only place – in the IBIS notation for opinion, clever rhetoric, and hand waving. Of course, it is preferable to have Arguments that provide factual assertions bearing on the advantages or disadvantages of an Idea. In the case of the toll-free number Idea, the supporting Argument would be, 'More inviting for customers to use.'

Examples of other Arguments:

- It's too expensive
- Will make the customer happy
- Not likely to be accepted by the marketplace
- Unreliable
- Costs 2.3 times more than the lowest cost model
- Performs beautifully
- Management won't go for it

The key to recognizing an Argument is that *Arguments give a reason for picking (or not picking) their Idea(s) as the best answer to the Question.*[5] If a statement makes you more likely to favor an Idea, then it's stating an argument for that idea: a Pro. If it makes you tend to disfavor the Idea, then it's a Con.

The IBIS method can considerably raise the quality of dialogue within a group or project team simply by concentrating all opinion into Argument nodes. For example, the old trick of 'truth by repetition' – saying one's point over and over until everyone else accedes – is disarmed, because once an Argument has been captured it becomes silly and obvious to repeat it. If someone restates an argument after it's been captured, the dialogue mapper can point to it in the map and ask, 'Do you mean this one again?' The speaker has less need to repeat his or her point once it is recorded; he or she knows the point has been heard and captured.

Being 'issue based,' IBIS is all about issues and questions. The main elements that tie a dialogue map together are the Questions in the map. The 'secret skill' at the heart of dialogue mapping is the art of finding the best questions. Any element in a map can have new Questions added to it – asking for more information, further detail, or challenging. For example, the Idea 'Build a new system' might have Questions connected to it that asked 'How to build it?,' 'How much would it cost?,' and 'How long would it take?'

This 'representational power' is why IBIS is such a good notation for wicked problems. IBIS cannot be overwhelmed with information that does not fit, or with too many questions or too many points of view. Dialogue maps can get very large. They can be messy or well organized – indeed, there's an aesthetic to well-formed maps. They can be nested many levels deep. There may be thousands of nodes in the maps for a project. But no one can ever say, 'We can't put that piece of knowledge in the system' or 'There's no good way to represent that point.'

Conversational Patterns

Now we can return to the mission statement conversation and explore the process of translating from 'everyday speak' to IBIS. In this section we will continue to 'dissect' the mission statement discussion into IBIS. Bear in mind that in a real meeting you probably wouldn't try to or even want to capture every single comment in the map. Our dissection exercise is to show how IBIS *can* capture anything being said.

After Sue's comment (captured as 'Best product, best price, outstanding service') the next statement was:

Tom: The main thing is that our computers have the best performance, so we should focus on that.

This one is a little trickier. Is Tom proposing that the mission statement should read 'Best performance,' or is he just suggesting that 'Best performance' should be a key part of the mission? We don't know for sure. Dialogue mapping is not about being psychic; rather it is about being willing to guess and to check the guess . . . and to be wrong sometimes. So we guess. Let's interpret his comment simply as another Idea about the mission statement:[6]

Best performance

Then Joe responds to Tom:

Joe: ZipCo's computers have superior performance to ours.

What is the 'logic' of this comment? It is meant to weaken the suggestion Tom just made, so it is an Argument against that Idea:

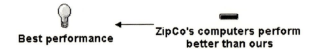

Best performance ← ZipCo's computers perform better than ours

Notice that we do not capture who said what. Once an Idea is in the map, it is just another idea, not 'Tom's idea.' Thus, in the map, *Joe is not disagreeing with Tom*. This makes it easier for the group to think critically together about all the possible options without getting into debate dynamics.

Directing the attention of the group a bit, you ask a question:

You: Shouldn't we say something about our concern for our employees?

It would be a mistake to capture this as a new Question in the map. The point of your comment is to offer another idea about the mission statement, so the dialogue mapper would simply capture it as an Idea, maybe:

Something about our concern for our employees

Sue picks up on your direction and takes it even further:

Sue: Yeah, and how about the fact that we are committed to being a green corporation, and contributing to society?

Again, stated as a question, but really just another idea (or possibly two):

Committed to being a green corporation, contributing to society

At this point, our dialogue map looks like Figure 4.5.

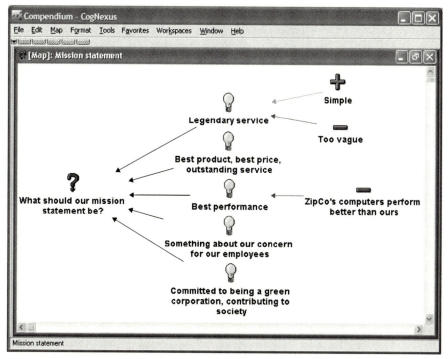

Figure 4.5   Dialogue map of the first part of the meeting

Note that some of the ideas are specific suggestions for a mission statement, while others are merely *about* the mission statement. At this point, it's OK to mix all these types of answer – we are just capturing and mapping the conversation. We are not trying to build a logic diagram or split hairs about semantics. The point here is just to get something in the map.

The next comment will help us show how IBIS helps us notice when a topic shift subtly occurs.

Joe: I still like, 'Legendary service.' It's simple. Why do we want it to be complex? No one will remember it.

First, Joe returns to his earlier idea, and adds new support, that it's 'easy to remember.' One way to capture this would simply be to tack it onto his supporting Argument that the idea was 'Simple,' thus:

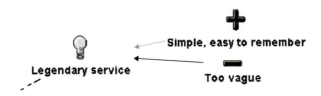

But if we listen a bit deeper, Joe is also raising a new issue. He shifted from *ideas* about the mission statement to *criteria* for a good mission statement. He is saying that *any* mission statement should be memorable. This would be captured as a new 'criterial' Question and its first Idea:

One of the conversational events that mires unmapped meetings in confusion is this kind of subtle shift of topic: one or several participants move on to a new issue while others are still back on the preceding issue. The result is literally two or more issues being discussed at the same time, the real problem with this is confusion about which comments are addressing which issue. Thus the skill of *hearing* when a new issue emerges and capturing it as a new Question in the map is key to using IBIS as a notation, as we will discuss in more detail in Chapter 6, 'Question Types.'

Opening up a new question is what IBIS is all about. Remember, IBIS stands for 'issue-based information system' – issues and questions are the basis, the nucleus around which everything else moves.

In the next statement, you make a process move to direct the flow of conversation:

You: Let's get everyone's input. What about you, Greg?

Since it's pure meeting process, this statement would not be captured in the map at all.

Greg: Well, I guess I don't understand what the purpose of the mission statement is. We're not talking about a position statement, that's marketing. I think the mission statement should have the employees be excited about the company they are working for.

Note the topic shift! Greg wants to talk about the *purpose* of the mission statement. Related topic, but distinct! In order to map Greg's comment the dialogue mapper has to start by getting the new Question into the map:

?

Purpose of mission statement?

Then, in the next sentence, 'We're not talking about a position statement, that's marketing,' Greg offers one answer to his question, and the support for his answer:

Not a position statement   **That's marketing**

Finally, Greg tells us what *he* thinks *is* the purpose of the mission statement:

Have employees be excited
about the company

So here is what Greg's comment looks like in IBIS:

As before, without the map Greg's move will occur as 'changing the subject' or 'straying from the agenda.' By catching the new Question this potentially disruptive move loses most of its negative connotation. As we shall explore more in Chapter 7 ('Three Moves of Discourse'), dialogue maps allow for a wide variety of conversational moves and learning styles, all of which are useful for the larger picture of the group's collective intelligence to emerge.

If Greg's comment seemed off the subject, Joe's response to it is what some people call 'grenade throwing':

Joe: If you want to do that, just increase everyone's salaries. Or at least give people better titles. People have been clamoring for that, and it doesn't even cost us anything.

In a typical meeting setting, this comment would set off a long diversion on salaries and titles, which would be off the subject, as well as old territory for most of the people present. Or the meeting leader might simply sidestep the comment, turning the group back to the mission statement, but leaving Joe's contribution completely unacknowledged. Dialogue mapping offers a third option: hear and capture the comment, and then use the map itself to draw everyone's energy back to the 'center of mass' . . . the discussion of the mission statement. This is the self-organizing power of collaborative display in action – we meet each person's contribution and capture it, and the display holds the overall structure of the conversation up like a mirror for the group to see the pattern of their conversation, and self-correct if necessary.

In this case, it would be very hard to take Joe's suggestion, 'just increase everyone's salaries,' and put it into the map as it stands. This is a common predicament in dialogue mapping:[7] what Joe said is very clearly an Idea . . . it just doesn't happen to connect to anything in the map!

Ideally, the trick – and it is indeed a matter of skill and luck – is to *hear the hidden Question* in the comment (discussed more in Chapter 6, 'Question Types'). But, if you can't tell right away what the hidden Question is, start with the Idea and work backward to the Question. In this case, the new Idea is clear:

Increase everyone's salaries

Maps don't always grow left to right – sometimes Ideas hang out for a while, waiting for their Question to become clear.

Since we're dissecting this conversation, we can take the time to figure out what Joe's hidden Question is. The clue is in the way he introduces it: 'If you want to do that [have employees be excited about the company] . . .' The hidden Question would be something like:

Joe also has another Idea on this same Question, and two supporting arguments for it:

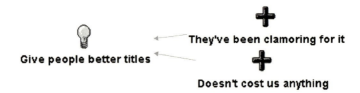

With the pieces pulled together, the IBIS version of Joe's 'diversion' is:

By capturing Joe's hidden Question in the map, we have:

- captured all of Joe's comments in a coherent way;
- shown how they relate to the preceding discussion;
- acknowledged Joe's contribution;
- opened a new issue that the group can choose to address or not, depending on their energy and time constraints.

At this point, a dialogue mapper might interrupt the conversation to validate what's been captured (Figure 4.6), and also to show the group that this new question about how to excite employees is a natural follow-on to the discussion of the criteria for the mission statement. It's not a problem for the map that Joe made this shift – it's not a 'grenade' in the conversation. The dialogue mapper has several options about how to link Joe's new Question into the rest of the map. But it's less critical whether and how it gets linked – links can easily be changed or added after the meeting.

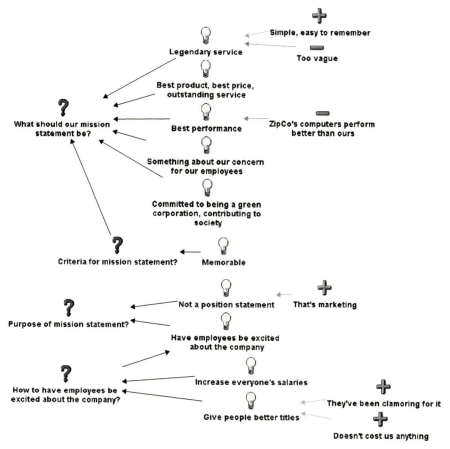

Figure 4.6 Dialogue map for the whole mission statement conversation

With Figure 4.6 we have built an IBIS map that represents the 'messy conversation' from the beginning of the chapter. This instructional exercise is meant to illustrate that *everything* that is spoken in a design conversation can be mapped in IBIS, and to introduce you to the 'how-to' of using IBIS in meetings.

Normally, however, the dialogue mapper would not try to capture the details of every comment – that would take too long and slow the group down without adding much value. (The art of what to capture and what to leave out of the map will be explored more in Chapter 5.) Figure 4.7 shows a much simpler and more likely map for the short segment of the meeting in our example – most of the side questions did not get captured in this version. Moreover, if this conversation really had been facilitated using dialogue mapping, it probably would have unfolded differently, more coherently. Conversations are always impacted by the use of a collaborative display and dialogue mapping.

Figure 4.7   A more likely map for the brief meeting segment in the example

The trick is to make sure that the impact on the conversation is welcomed and beneficial. If you focus on being of service and listening to everyone without adding any of your own agenda, you will always be adding value to a conversation. Think of IBIS and the map as 'props' to help you listen and add value.

Benefits of IBIS

Let's step back a moment and consider . . . do we really need IBIS? Maybe all you need to create shared understanding is a shared display and a good note taker. What if you just created a diagram of people's points as they spoke, drawing a line from each point to any related points, as in Figure 4.8?

That approach might work fine . . . for a while. But if the meeting went on for a couple of hours, the diagram would eventually become

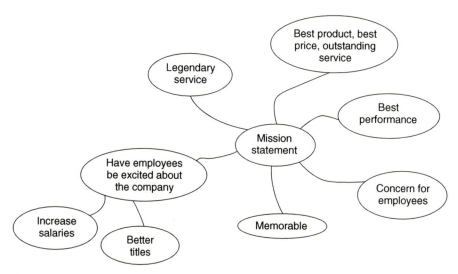

Figure 4.8 Concept map of mission statement discussion

a big tangle of balloons and string. It would be hard to tell what was where and what the lines meant. The cleanup process would involve many arbitrary decisions about how to 'chunk' the diagram into smaller sub-diagrams. You would also have problems if there were any serious disagreements during the meeting – how would you diagram the debate? (And what project meeting lacks disagreement, or at least creative tension?)

If, instead of a free-form diagramming technique, you used the IBIS elements to diagram the conversation, that would be dialogue mapping. IBIS provides *just enough* structure to allow the diagrams to keep growing indefinitely. Sure, in practice you need to clean maps up and reorganize them from time to time, but this is much easier with IBIS because everything is organized by Questions. The map in Figure 4.6 has 20 nodes, but they are organized into just four Questions, each with its discussion. Keeping track of what has been said and where it's captured in the map is much easier, for the same reason.

Thus one major benefit of IBIS is that it provides a structure in which all the twisty turns of problem solving discussions can be modeled. In short, IBIS functions as a grammar.

In English, you cannot say 'John ball hit the.' English grammar forbids it. In IBIS, maps never start with an Argument node, for example, neither are Arguments allowed to object to Questions. The IBIS notation imposes a discipline on dialogue maps, with two complementary consequences: it is harder to learn to use IBIS than to use free-form techniques, and IBIS maps are more rigorous, more robust, and more reproducible. When dealing with wicked problems, this additional structure is essential to maintaining coherence as maps grow.

Since chunking a big map into several smaller, more manageable ones is a frequent operation, the Compendium mapping software makes this operation easy. Often, the signal for a new chunk, a new map, is a major new question. For example, in Figure 4.6, the exploration of the purpose of the mission statement might lead to a larger and more detailed argument structure that would be better moved into its own map (Figure 4.9). This new 'sub-map' would be hyperlinked to the top-level map.

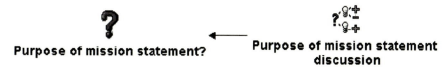

Purpose of mission statement? ← **Purpose of mission statement discussion**

Figure 4.9   Discussion of a Question has been moved into a sub-map

In addition to structural coherence, IBIS invokes a discipline of finding the right questions and making strong cases. Recall that 'IBIS' stands for *'issue-based* information system.' Issues, stated as questions, are the heart of this method. One benefit of asking questions in a collaborative situation is that it helps to break up the 'answer reflex,' in which participants exchange answers without ever agreeing on the question. By getting a group (or an individual!) to think in terms of questions you encourage higher quality thinking and reasoning.

It is also much easier to see the substance of a debate when it is mapped out in IBIS . . . and, indeed, to tell if there *is* any substance. If there are several Ideas, but only one has any Arguments, the map begs for additional Pros and Cons on the other Ideas. In fact all kinds of questionable logic and hand waving, which can slip by in spoken interaction, are revealed quite clearly when laid out in IBIS. Indeed, many people who have learned dialogue mapping have never facilitated a single meeting – they use their understanding of IBIS to think about and map out issues such as where to move, whether to go back to school or look for a new job, or what renovations to do on the house.

As we'll see in Chapter 6, there are seven *types* of question in IBIS. These question types connect together in higher level patterns, or templates. These patterns provide additional order and reproducibility in IBIS maps. For example, there are factual questions, such as 'What is the performance of the competitors' products?' There are deontic questions, such as 'What should our mission statement be?' There are instrumental questions, such as 'How can we increase sales?' Each type of question has certain kinds of answers, and they fit together in regular patterns of reasoning.

A third benefit of the IBIS notation is that it is simple and intuitive. Several studies have shown that the potential advantages of notations like IBIS are often offset by the increased 'cognitive overhead' of applying them 'on the fly' . . . when you are engaged in a substantive task (Buckingham Shum and Hammond, 1994). In part, this overhead imposes a constraint on the expressive power of any formalism that might be adopted in problem solving or design process: candidate notations must be simple and intuitive enough that the 'cognitive cost' of using them is very low. Years of practical experience have shown that more sophisticated and expressively powerful notations than IBIS are much more difficult to apply in a transparent way. IBIS is just complex enough to be able to handle wicked problems, just simple enough to be practical for meeting capture.

There is another way to meet the challenge of 'cognitive overhead,' and that is to recognize that lowering the cognitive cost of use is in part a matter of *fluency*. Although English is generally recognized as one of the more difficult languages to learn in the world, fluent speakers are unaware of the 'cognitive overhead' of English when they are engaged in discussion. English is transparent to both speakers and listeners who are fluent. Similarly, as with a language or a musical instrument, practice and fluency render IBIS both transparent and powerful.

As simple as IBIS is, it can be broken down even further to increase its simplicity for those in the learning phase. One part of IBIS is Questions and Ideas/answers, the basic constituents of dialogue dating back to Aristotle. Virtually anyone can listen to a debate and quickly discern what the question is (or questions are), and what the positions or possible answers are. Moreover, the majority of comments in an analytic discussion are questions and answers, so you can map much of these interactions using only these two IBIS elements.

More challenging for IBIS students is the proper use of Arguments, the pros and cons for the various Ideas. Of course, the *concept* of Arguments is simple and intuitive. Most people are quite used to thinking in terms of tradeoffs, benefits and disadvantages, strengths and weaknesses, opportunities and threats, and so on. These are the basic terms of critical analysis. However, there are subtle pitfalls for the unpracticed. For example, a Pro for the Idea 'Increase everyone's salaries' might be 'Will decrease turnover.' Even though lowering employee turnover clearly supports the Idea to increase salaries, it is tempting for beginners to make this a Con because 'decrease' and 'turnover' somehow *feel* negative. In applying Arguments clearly and correctly a background in logic can come in handy!

In any case, it turns out that only about 10% of the nodes in open-ended and exploratory discussions are Argument nodes, and even fewer in more structured analyses (Selvin and Sierhuis, 1999), so in most situations these are the least important of the IBIS elements.

Distinguishing the three basic elements of IBIS – Questions, Ideas, and Arguments – can become, with practice, very natural. Indeed, many people report that, having learned IBIS, they find it very frustrating to listen to discussions in which the participants are not making these basic rhetorical distinctions! Moreover, participants in meetings in which IBIS mapping is done on the fly, either with markers on a whiteboard or with software on a computer projector, find the notation quite natural and obvious. No explanation is necessary, and any sense of mystery about what is going on generally vanishes quickly – assuming, of course, some level of fluency in the person doing the mapping!

In addition to how simple and natural this notation is, it is also important to convey the *power* of IBIS as a mapping notation for complex analyses. It is easiest to see this power simply by reflecting on what happens *without* such a notation. Different players have different ideas about what the issue is, especially in a wicked problem. Each player addresses their comments to *their version* of the issue, but it is often unclear how many versions of the issue there are, or what they are. Making the issues explicit in an IBIS map adds a tremendous clarity to the discussion, as does being clear about which of those issues a given comment is addressing. Wicked problems often have dozens of interrelated issues involved, but human short-term memory is very limited, so unless one is extremely familiar with all the information related to all of the issues, the unaided exploration of these issues is confusing and error prone. The power of IBIS as a notation is that it organizes the issues, positions, information, and assumptions so that all participants have the issue map as a point of reference, and they can refer to it instead of trying to keep it all in their head. Thus IBIS contributes to dialogue mapping being a force for coherence because it augments human cognition at one of its weakest points: the limits of short-term memory.

To summarize the benefits of IBIS, then:

- It offers 'structural coherence' to the record of a design or problem-solving conversation, organized by Questions that are arranged from high level (most general) issues down to any level of low level (most specific and detailed) issues.
- IBIS reinforces a discipline of making substantive, rational cases in favor of or against the main options on any decisions, thus providing a more consistent, transparent, and democratic environment for collaborative work.
- It is simple and intuitive to learn and to use.
- It has enough representational power to capture any design or problem-solving interaction.

Gaining Fluency in IBIS

A young man is walking down a street in New York. 'Excuse me,' he says to an older woman as they pass, 'how can I get to Carnegie Hall?' The woman stops, looks at him firmly, shakes her finger and says, 'There's only one way! Practice! Practice! Practice!'

At this point, dear reader, you may be thinking that IBIS is not as 'simple' and 'intuitive' as you had hoped, and that your project meetings are maybe just fine the way they are.

Don't worry . . . actually, you now know enough to start dialogue mapping today! I recommend it, in fact. Go find a friend, colleague, or family member, get a 'shared display' (a piece of paper will do), and write down the main question that you want to think about together. As anyone makes a new point, find a way to put it into your dialogue map. Make sure that your partner can see and understand your writing. That's all there is to it!

Nearly all there is, anyway. If you picked a really hard problem it's likely that you quickly reached a point where the comment that had just been made didn't fit in the map – it wasn't a Question, it wasn't an Idea, and it wasn't an Argument. Don't despair! Did I mention this takes practice?

Actually, we have just described the practice paradox: simple ('tame') problems don't require dialogue mapping to get to a solution; and wicked problems require skillful dialogue mapping just to get to a workable statement of the problem! It's like the loan paradox: you can only get a loan if you don't need one. To get the confidence and skill you need to stand up in front of your colleagues and dialogue map their discussion about whether to create and launch a new product, you need practice with problems that could be solved without the map.

Remember that speaking and listening in everyday English is actually an incredibly complex and highly skilled activity, and yet you do it without giving it any thought. IBIS is a language, like English, but much, much simpler. You are fluent in English, but not IBIS. Being able to discern coherence in a wicked problem, or being able to facilitate a diverse group through a highly charged and political discussion, is a matter of fluency in listening and writing in the IBIS language, combined with grace in the dance of crafting a dialogue map with a group.

With IBIS fluency, charged and tangled discussions become transparent: you can see the hidden questions, and you can hear that the debate is heated because the participants are trying to answer different questions. You can detect when someone 'throws a grenade' in the conversation, but it doesn't cause you any angst because you can literally see the move in the map, and show it to the group. You can support people in making clear and compelling cases for and against different ideas, because you are hearing the arguments and the case making.

Following the fluency metaphor, what dialogue mapping provides is a tool or language for a new kind of literacy: *collaborative literacy*. Literacy means being educated, cultured, being able to read and write, having knowledge or competence. Collaborative literacy means having an education in collaboration, having a set of distinctions and skills that allow one to be a powerful agent for collective intelligence and collaborative effectiveness. Collaborative literacy comes the same way any kind of literacy comes, from education and practice. The more situations in which you practice, the faster you become comfortable with it . . . fluent in it.

Broadly speaking, there are three clearly discernable stages in gaining IBIS fluency. In the first stage, you are learning the basic IBIS notation. You can translate a written text into an IBIS map, but it takes a few minutes and you may stumble or get stuck a couple of times. This is probably where you are.

With practice you enter the second stage: you know the IBIS grammar, the conversational building blocks, and you are beginning to see some common patterns. You know the basic steps of the collaborative display dance, but you're not really comfortable with the dance when the discussion gets hot. You can generally listen to someone speaking and capture most of their points on the fly in IBIS, although sometimes your maps get a bit twisted and need some effort to be 'repaired.' You are no longer afraid of large dialogue maps. You understand the power of collaborative display, and you are comfortable with the 'listening cycle' of listening–guessing–writing–validating (covered in the next chapter).

In the third stage you are fluent in IBIS and skillful in dialogue mapping. You 'hear' Questions, Ideas, Pros, and Cons as they are spoken, and you often can anticipate what is coming next. You see how sets of questions cascade together in design conversations. Indeed, you have a sense that there is really just one 'master pattern' for all design and planning conversations, and each meeting is just a matter of creating a particular dialogue map according to this master pattern. You are a master dialogue mapper and are comfortable guiding a group through their wicked problem using the shared display.

It's just a matter of 'practice, practice, practice.' As you practice with other people, remember not to get hung up on getting the IBIS structure perfect. Think of learning to play the piano. Alone you struggle to get the notes exactly right. Performing for others, you try to make music.

Here are some simple ways to get more practice as you start out:

- Privately map out a problem you are working on, one that matters to you (e.g. new job? move? new car?).

- Have a 'meeting' with a friend or family member about a problem you both care about and map out the conversation.
- Watch a TV sitcom and map out the 'issues' in the plot. (Easy!)
- Watch a TV news analysis show and map out the discussion of the issues. (Hard!)
- Analyze a newspaper or magazine article in IBIS.
- Privately map the group dialogue when you attend meetings.

If you are using Compendium to create IBIS maps, you might want to try separating some of your IBIS practice from your software skills practice. These are two very distinct skills, using different parts of the brain, and practicing them both together can make the practice extra difficult. It can even slow you down in gaining IBIS fluency. Use pencil and paper for some of your IBIS practice sessions, so you can focus on the wording and the structure.

Here is another tip: read a little in this book, practice a little, then read some more, then practice some more. You might even want to reread this whole book after you get some real practice sessions under your belt.

Notes

1. Rittel, 1972a, p. 394.
2. All of the screenshots in this book are taken from Compendium. See Appendix.
3. Strictly speaking, IBIS is a *grammar* – a set of simple rules for building IBIS diagrams – but we'll use the more comfortable term *notation* here.
4. There is a variety of formats for writing IBIS. Since Compendium is the de facto standard tool for dialogue mapping, we will show IBIS dialogue maps as they appear in Compendium. For a discussion of other

notations, see the *Dialogue Mapping without a Computer* section in this chapter.

5. The IBIS notation allows an Argument to support or object to more than one Idea, but it is not that common in practice, partly because it is often cleaner to restate a Pro or Con precisely for each Idea.

6. In a real meeting we would validate our guess with the speaker: 'Like this?' or 'Is this right?'

7. In normal conversation, people often shift the topic, not by asking a new question – that would be too obvious – but by injecting an idea that doesn't fit the old question.

5
The Dialogue Mapping Listening Cycle

Dialogue mapping is like speaking a foreign language and dancing at the same time. IBIS is the language. The dance step is called the 'listening cycle.' The listening cycle is the heart of the collaborative display dance – it is the key to shifting from the role of scribe or note taker to dialogue mapper. As you practice with IBIS to develop fluency, you will also need to deliberately practice the listening cycle . . . to develop rhythm.

When you are learning a new dance step, you follow the numbered shoe prints on the floor. When you are *dancing* . . . there are no shoe prints, there aren't even steps to follow. There is just the dance. In the same way, once you get the natural call-and-response rhythm of the listening cycle, you never think about it again.
But in the early phases of learning it helps to know the steps.

Don't Just Stand There – Write Something!

One of the most exhilarating experiences in dialogue mapping is finding yourself listening to the point someone is saying and translating into IBIS and typing or writing it – all at the same time. Fortunately, it's not necessary to start at this level of performance – the process works just fine if you listen to the comment, and then type it.

The challenge for novice dialogue mappers is the compelling desire to *wait to write until they have thoroughly understood the speaker's meaning*. Unfortunately, if you wait until each speaker is clear about what they are trying to say, you may still be waiting at the end of the meeting!

The first key to success in Dialogue Mapping is to jump in and start capturing right away.

That way, you've got *something* up in the display as each new move in the conversation begins, and the group sees that you are still there, following the conversation closely, a stake in the ground. This is listening with an edge, listening that doesn't let up.

What I Meant to Say Is . . .

We're all familiar with active listening: you listen to someone and then echo back in your own words what you heard him or her say. Dialogue mapping is active listening on steroids: you listen to someone and then echo back what you heard them say on a giant computer screen. It is impossible for someone *not* to feel listened to if you do this. The speaker gets the clear message that they are being heard, and that what they say matters – everyone's speaking is honored in this environment. Each speaker also gets assistance with getting his or her meaning across.

How often have you heard someone make a statement, and then say, 'What I mean is . . .' and make a completely different statement? Saying what you mean is not easy. If the topic is complex, or poorly understood, or emotionally loaded, it is rare that the first attempt at expressing a new idea is a complete success. Sometimes there is a 'rambling' quality as a speaker tries to find the right words. Some-times someone else interrupts and the speaker never finishes his or her thought. In any case, meaning is not made and then delivered. *Meaning is being created as it is being spoken.* Sense making happens in the dance of speaking and listening.

The listening cycle provides a structure in which the capture process supports this meaning-making process, and assures that what is cap-tured in the map is the best possible representation of the intended meaning.

Ideally, the dialogue mapper tries to write down the *essence* of what the speaker is saying – capturing it verbatim if possible. Since people often say more than is essential to express their point, you try to *summarize* or *paraphrase* it. Getting the written paraphrase up in the collaborative display is important for several reasons:

- It is faster to write than the whole comment, and therefore leaves more time for capturing the next comment.
- It is faster to read, and thus easier for the speaker to review and validate.

- Your paraphrase reflects back to the speaker what their words mean to someone else, which can help the speaker get out what they are really trying to say.

Of course, you cannot possibly write what someone is saying at the exact moment they are saying it. You will always be behind. The question is . . . how behind should you be? At one end of the spectrum you can try to type as fast as the speaker talks. At the other end you can listen, paraphrase back to the speaker verbally, and then type it if they agree with your paraphrase. The latter is tempting, because if you follow closely the speaker sometimes tells you that your written paraphrase is completely wrong and you have to erase it and start over. But if you wait until the end and echo back your paraphrase verbally, if the speaker says, 'Yes, that's it,' you have another problem – you've got a lot of typing to do before you can concentrate on listening to the next speaker. So somewhere in the middle of this spectrum is best: start typing when you get an idea of what they are saying, and when they finish speaking type the rest of it.

Guessing and Validating

Close observation of very skilled dialogue mappers reveals that they are doing a bit more than just listening and writing. They are actually going through a four-step process. Whether they are consciously aware of it or not, their use of this 'listening cycle' makes them appear to be masterful in practice. The four steps are listen, guess, write, and validate (see Figure 5.1). Before the cycle starts the dialogue mapper selects *one person* to attend to.

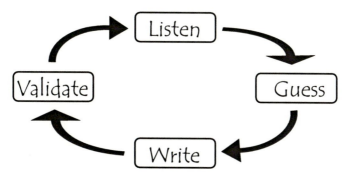

Figure 5.1 Dialogue mapping listening cycle

Listen to what the person is saying. If several people are speaking, that's OK – pick one and pay attention to him.

Guess what he is trying to say. Sometimes this is easy. He said 'That won't work' and you can write down 'That won't work.' Sometimes it is not so clear what the speaker is trying to say. There may be pauses, restarts, grammatical ambiguity, words you don't know . . . or maybe it just doesn't make sense to you. That's OK – take whatever you do get and go with it. Trust yourself. Make a guess. Don't wait for the speaker to finish crafting a clear, complete statement. Actively pursue your interpretation of what he is trying to say.

Write down your guess as soon as you have one. You can tune it and adjust it as you write – guessing and writing are really the same process. Write down the essence of his thought, or what the essence seems to you at that moment.

Validate your guess with the speaker. If everyone's eyes are glued to the shared display screen, this may be as simple as momentary eye contact. If the speaker is looking at someone else, you may need to interrupt to get him to glance at the screen, read what you've written, and indicate whether or not he is happy with your version.

It is important to understand how different this listening cycle is from the common wisdom about listening. Common wisdom is that you wait until the speaker is finished, and you assume that they said precisely what they meant. When dealing with wicked and ill-structured problems, however, it is rarely the case that anyone is really certain about what they mean. Your job as dialogue mapper is to be a partner with the speaker, actively encouraging them on, and helping them with the difficult job of crafting a clear statement about an unclear topic.

The second success factor in dialogue mapping is knowing that *interrupting is OK if you do it in the service of listening*. If you have taken the trouble to write down a paraphrase of what someone is trying to say, it will almost always be fine with them if you jump in to ask if you got it right. This is one of the hardest parts of the listening cycle for people to really get, especially if they are shy or have been raised to be very polite. The socialization to not interrupt is intense, and that socialization can seriously impede your ability to serve a group that is wrestling with a wicked problem. *It is essential to interrupt!* It reminds the group that you and the display are still there, and that you really care about what they are saying. It establishes the collaborative display as the ultimate arbiter of validity – a point is valid if it is captured in the display. (One very skilled practitioner brazenly announces to his groups, 'If it's not in the map, it didn't happen!') And in cases of tension or debate, it breaks the spell of combat, and releases the participants from their basal instincts for fight or flight.

Besides, with many groups, if you don't interrupt – if you just wait patiently for a pause in the discussion to make your validation move – you may end up with an unvalidated map. In fact, it can easily happen that the group barely noticed that you were mapping. Trust me – this is not a fun way to do dialogue mapping! (Unless you are *practicing* listening and capture in IBIS! This can be a terrific way to get practice.)

Summarizing and Paraphrasing

Here's an example of using the listening cycle. Let's take a single statement and dissect its capture in detail.

You are dialogue mapping for a management team at Acme Household Services, and there's been a presentation proposing that the company move into diaper recycling as a new service offering. You have captured the proposal as the Idea 'Diaper recycling.' Then one of the managers says:

You know, here's my concern about this proposal. It seems to me we tried something like this before, and I'm pretty sure that others have tried it. But we have to consider the realities of our situation here. I'm not saying it can't be done . . . And I would certainly echo John's desire that we get something laid out pretty soon, so that people can start to react to it . . . But money doesn't grow on trees, and we're the group folks are looking at to set a new fiscal example. It just seems to me that this idea is too ambitious and too risky. I mean, what if it flops?

If you are a lightning typist, you might put this whole statement in the detail[1] of a node. But most of us will be happier if this statement gets boiled down a bit. (Including the speaker, who might be stricken if he looked up and saw this whole rambling text captured on the screen!)

What has the speaker really said? What is the essence of his concern? How would you represent it in IBIS?

It isn't necessary to know what kind of move this statement is in IBIS before you write something, but with practice it will be easy and natural to make guesses about the kind of move the speaker is making as well as the content. Just from his use of the word 'concern,' you know the group is about to hear a possible problem with the proposed Idea, a reason not to do it . . . a 'Con' in the IBIS vernacular. So you can create that node type right away.

How would you paraphrase this comment for the node label? Here are some possible summaries of the statement, and some comments on them (Box 5.1).

Box 5.1 Statement summaries and comments

'Too risky'	This is the one I would use, with 'Too ambitious' in the detail to clarify the risk
'Too ambitious'	Also fine, especially with 'Too risky' in the detail
'Too risky/ambitious'	Very good. Combining several words together using a / can be a fast way to capture the sense of a statement without struggling to pick the 'right' word. Such 'slashifying' avoids unnecessary struggles over minor terminology differences

'We tried it before'	Captures a *potential* concern, but not the essence of the comment. It may be that they tried it before and it worked out OK. This would become an objection if he had said 'We tried that before and it didn't work'
	If you made this as an early guess, you would just replace it when it became clear that he was making a different argument
'Money doesn't grow on trees'	Captures the objection, but not as directly as 'Too risky'
	You might have guessed 'Too expensive' – that would be a good guess, and one that you would validate with the speaker. But you still need another objecting Argument about the risk. (It is fine to capture several nodes from one comment – points are often bundled together in a single statement)
'What if it flops?'	This one would be tempting, because it is how he ended his comments. I think it is probably a rhetorical question meant to emphasize the risk issue. If you capture it as a Question, you are inviting the group to speculate about the consequences if the proposal fails. If you

feel the group wants or needs to explore this issue, a better phrasing would be 'Consequences of failure?' as a new Question linked to the Idea. But first get the Con (e.g. 'Too risky') captured in the map. If you also capture the new question, be prepared for a whole new turn in the conversation

Obviously, how you paraphrase a long comment like this is a matter of personal style and preference, and it's not a critical moment in the process because, if you get it wrong, the speaker will tell you! Just listening and writing *something* in the shared display will contribute to improving the communication process.

Riding the Cycle

Let's go through the example comment on p. 129 in a bit more detail as you, the dialogue mapper, work through the listening cycle. As this manager is speaking you are *listening* to him, considering possible

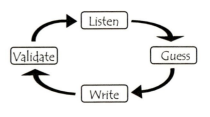

interpretations of his comment as it unfolds. With practice, you are using IBIS to help you see the deep structure of the conversation, and anticipating the kind of move that he is most likely to be making (see Chapter 7, 'Three Moves of Discourse', for more on some common moves people make in meetings). And you are *guessing* about which interpretation is most central to his 'communicative intent'.

As soon as you have a guess, you start *writing*. Let's say you write 'Too risky' as an objection linked back to the idea (see Figure 5.2). The moment you are done typing you look at the speaker. You might say to him 'Is that it?' or 'Did I get it?' If he looks at you, you glance at the screen. You watch his face. If he nods or says 'Yes' you have *validated* your capture and completed the cycle. It's time to pick someone else and go through the listening cycle with them.

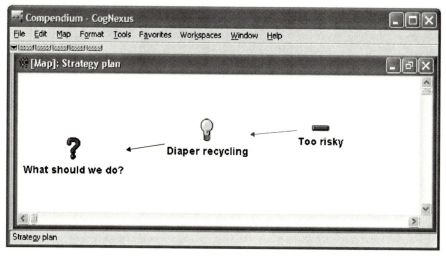

Figure 5.2 First guess

If he says 'No' you are back to the listening step – be ready to immediately delete what you have written, and start listening to his clarification. It is essential to be totally unattached to the guess you wrote. He may be saying that you missed his point, or he may be acknowledging that he hasn't made his point clear yet. You are his partner – your job is to be a transparent vehicle of meaning capture. As he speaks again, he'll be using your first guess as a signal to be clearer, to tune his meaning, to find another way to say his point. He might say:

It's not necessarily too risky – that depends on how we implement it – but I don't think there are any cost-effective methods for recycling dirty diapers.

That's a shorter comment . . . and a different point! You might write 'No cost-effective recycling methods' as the new label of your Con (see Figure 5.3).

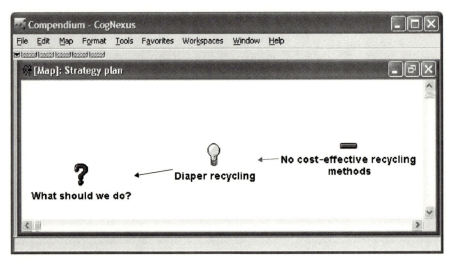

Figure 5.3 Second try

Sometimes it works to say the phrase you are going to write before typing it. Before typing you might say 'Ahhh, there are "No-cost effective recycling methods" for dirty diapers,' and then start typing the new label.

If so, it's good practice to start typing your guess as soon as you have said it. Or, you can enter a one-on-one conversation with the speaker on crafting the best possible paraphrase of their comment. The two of you might go back and forth verbally several times. In this way you are recruiting the group into helping you create good paraphrases. Usually they will get the idea and, when someone has finished a comment, they'll look right at you and say, 'That would be "Too ambitious".'

Got Rhythm?

It may look like the dialogue mapper is doing all the work, but actually you are training the group to speak precisely, listen deeply, and engage in an intense and deliberate communication process. As the group gets accustomed to the process, the display, and your mapping style – as they get trained to participate in dialogue mapping – the process gets easier, more comfortable, and more fun.

One of the most profound aspects of the listening cycle is that it creates a rhythm. You and the group enter an almost tribal condition of working together to the steady beat of an invisible drum. Someone speaks, you listen→guess→write→validate, someone else speaks, you listen→guess→write→validate. Everything that is said fits into the rhythm and goes into the map. Call. Response. Call. Response.

In the beginning, people will continue their usual behavior . . . talking one after another, interrupting each other, barely waiting for one person to finish their point so the next can make his. But, the more you repeat the listening cycle, with one dance partner at a time, the more group members get conditioned to wait their turn, knowing when it comes to them, they will also get fully heard. Dissenters will know to add cons to the map. Advocates will add pros. People taking notes will look up at the screen and see that you've captured points they didn't even hear.

Over time, your participants will get trained . . . and entrained! . . . to your rhythmic repetition of the listening cycle. They will expect you to write what they're saying, and to confirm what you wrote. The more you repeat the listening cycle, one dance partner at a time, the better trained the group becomes. A satisfying rhythm gets established between the map and the participants. The combination of the listening cycle and the IBIS syntax will encourage the participants to clarify immediately, to begin to separate issues from ideas from reasons. This greatly increases the collaborative effectiveness of the group and reduces·spurious conflict.

Some people will get it right away, others will insist on being explicitly asked to validate every time they speak. That's really OK. You are the bridge to the collaborative display. Every time you speak you are entering the flow of the discussion, and every time you look or wave at the screen you are boosting the importance and ownership of the collaborative display in the meeting.

Capturing in Conversational Chunks

A few pages ago I said that the spectrum of time before capture ranged from typing *as* someone is speaking to waiting until they are done and *then* capturing it. Unfortunately, it is not that simple. The real range extends to waiting until a whole group topic or segment is done before capturing it. But the longer you wait to write something, the more catching up you are setting yourself up for. If you wait until the group has thoroughly discussed a whole topic, and there is a natural pause, you are likely to have forgotten half of what was said. At this point you have a choice: accept that some portion of the conversation is not captured and keep on going to the next topic, or stop the group and ask them to help you construct the missed portion of the map. Reconstructing a conversation in order to map it can be a surprisingly effective way to engage a group in the mapping process. By the same token, in my experience, you can't play this card very often.

Similarly, if you capture a segment but don't validate it, it's your choice when (and if) it gets validated. It often depends on the kind of meeting and the importance of accuracy and completeness of what's captured in the map. Regardless of your choice of timing, you can still use the listening cycle. If you let the conversation go on for several minutes without validating the map, you write what you can and then ask the group to validate that section of the map.

It's all about memory. A major benefit of the collaborative display is to create group memory. But the process relies critically on your personal memory as the mapper. You have to find the best granularity of capture and the best rhythm of validation, for a particular group and type of meeting. Follow too close and you won't be able to write it all. Too far behind and you won't remember it all.

The good news is, anything that you miss, you can simply ask the group to help you recall it. You look at the display, walk through the IBIS nodes that you captured, and ask, 'Was there anything else? Did I miss anything?'

So far it sounds like the only right way to do dialogue mapping is to capture and validate 100% of the conversation. It's not that simple.

I have mapped an entire meeting without once validating the map. The meeting was in Washington, DC, and every participant in the meeting was at least a one-star general in the military. I captured many of the points they were making in the map, and at the end of the meeting we provided each general with a printout of the map.

I have no idea if they ever looked at it. They certainly did not have any ownership of it. I *think* some of them noticed that I was typing away during the meeting, and some may have noticed things happening on the big bright computer screen at the front of the room. But I did not have the courage to interrupt them to validate even once. I kept waiting for the chance, but it never came. I didn't authorize myself to get them to include the collaborative display. And I'm pretty sure that the map did not improve their meeting.

But it didn't hurt the meeting, and it may have been a useful record for some. I suspect that the real purpose of their meeting was not on the agenda; it wasn't to make a decision or solve a problem. The purpose of their meeting, I think, was to sort out power dynamics and social relationships. This is a totally valid purpose for a meeting, but it's a purpose that dialogue mapping isn't very good at serving.[2] (See Chapter 8 for a further discussion of the limits of dialog mapping.)

At the end of the day, the value of dialogue mapping in any given session depends on many factors, only some of which are under your control: your level of mastery of dialogue mapping, the collaborative intent of the group, the urgency and complexity of the problem, the group leader's preparation and level of engagement, the physical layout of the room and the computer display, and many other factors.

The best you can ever do is to sincerely intend to add as much value as possible to the collaborative effort.

Intellectual Integrity

When a group needs to make a decision or solve a problem, dialogue mapping raises the group's intellectual integrity, in the sense of being unimpaired, whole and complete. The conversation is on record. What each person says matters. Everyone participates in the construction of the dialogue map, and everyone has ownership of it as their collective work product.

Integrity can be fun. The dialogue mapping experience can make meetings about complex subjects enjoyable, because the complexity of the topic does not defeat the process of clear and effective communication. Everything is getting said, and – more important – everything is also being heard. And validated. And captured. Even if *nothing* is agreed on, and 17 new hard problems surface during the meeting, the simple act of participating in this rhythmic ritual of group process can have the participants leave feeling good about what they accomplished together. They worked hard at surfacing those 17 issues, and they have the map to show for it.

The listening cycle helps ensure the intellectual integrity of the map – it ensures a complete and faithful representation of the conceptual territory covered during the meeting. Not just action items, but also open issues, decisions made, and newly surfaced assumptions. All relevant points are captured and woven together in a way that preserves context and makes sense to the participants.

Naturally, you print the map out for the participants at the end of the meeting. (The Appendix has links to discussions and documents about how to create meeting notes documents in Compendium.) Naturally, you have the map available at the next session, and you probably review it or parts of it as a way to refresh the group memory.

Learning the Listening Cycle

You can practice and use the listening cycle without doing a whit of dialogue mapping. The listening cycle is universal – it is the key to effective collaborative display of any kind in any setting.

To practice the cycle you don't need IBIS at all. Making a list of brainstormed ideas on a flipchart will be more effective if you are using the listening cycle. Crafting the wording of a press release with a group of marketing executives will work better if, in addition to using a word processor projected on a screen, you employ the listening cycle. So will filling out a budget spreadsheet with a group of division directors, or creating a presentation with a project team. In every case the point is to get the group to engage with the content of the display, giving it their full attention, and working together to produce the best possible product.

The way to really master the listening cycle is to take every opportunity to be at the keyboard when a group is collaborating to produce something . . . a brainstormed list, a press release, a budget, a presentation . . . anything at all. Once you get the knack of leading a group rhythm, you can combine the listening cycle with your knowledge of IBIS and, voilà!, you are dialogue mapping.

Experienced Facilitators: Read This!

If you've not had much facilitation experience it may be easier for you to pick up dialogue mapping, especially the listening cycle. Professional facilitators have learned a technique that they have to *unlearn* in order to get the listening cycle to work: They've learned to ask the group what it thinks or feels.

Dialogue mapping is different. The listening cycle is with *one person*, not the group. You pick *one speaker* to focus on and go through the cycle with him or her. You may go through the cycle several times with that person to get their point or points in the map. Then someone else with something to say will speak up, and you'll focus on them and go through the cycle with them. If several people try to speak at once, it's no problem: You pick one of them and attend to him or her.

If your validation move sounds like, 'What do *we* think?' or you hear yourself saying 'Does everybody agree with this idea?' you have slipped out of dialogue mapping. Yes, at the macro level the map is about what the whole group thinks. But *it is essential to the success of this process that, at the micro level, every cycle is about what one person thinks*. Validate your understanding or capture with one person and then, when they're done, pick the next person.

Most professional facilitators have been forced to compensate for working with an impoverished display and an underpowered notation. If there is disagreement about a point, they have to stop writing until the whole group agrees on the point, because most notations have no capacity to represent debate or disagreement. So facilitators have had to learn that you don't write anything down until the whole group agrees with it, i.e. 'Does everybody agree with this idea?' In practice, that means that if the problem is wicked, or the group is socially complex, nothing gets written down. There are too many issues and too much argumentation for anything to ever reflect the whole group's thinking.

That's why dialogue mapping is a breakthrough for modern collaborative efforts. It is a vehicle rich enough, a container strong enough, to handle the fragmenting forces of wicked problems and social complexity.

But . . . you may have to break some old habits to use it effectively.

Transcriptive versus Interpretive Capture

As with sports and the arts, dialogue mapping involves a fast-running stream of moment-by-moment choices. As someone speaks, you are choosing how you will capture their comment: how much detail to include, what IBIS elements to use, where and how to put them in the map, and how to validate. You may also be making choices about who to attend to, or other possible facilitation moves you might want to make.

Let's consider the range of options about what you capture. One option is to try to capture exactly, word for word, what someone is saying. This is called 'transcriptive capture,' because your intent is to create a transcript of the conversation. Obviously, you'll need to be a very good typist to even attempt being transcriptive.

On some occasions being transcriptive is straightforward. There is a direct question on the floor and in the map, like 'How to replace our inventory control system?' and someone says, 'Buy a new one.' You write down 'Buy a new one' in an Idea node. You don't have to wonder if you got it right, and you don't need to validate what you captured with the speaker. (And you might validate it anyway, because of the power of validation to orient the group to the collaborative display.)

More often, it is impossible to be completely transcriptive. People are talking too fast to capture it all. So you must be interpretive – you must interpret what you are hearing and find ways to paraphrase and summarize it in the text that you write. This is when the listening cycle is especially important. You write down your guess – your interpretation – and then you validate it with the speaker; if you misinterpreted, you'll find out quickly.

In fact, it often isn't even desirable to be transcriptive. Let's say you have the question about the inventory control system up on the screen, and someone says, 'You know, it's funny that we're talking about this, because just yesterday I had lunch with a guy from LeaseCo, and he was telling me about the benefits of leasing software systems. It's pretty interesting. I had never even really considered it before.'

You might surmise that he is suggesting leasing as an option, so you write down, 'Lease new system' and ask the speaker, 'So, we should consider leasing, right?' Most likely he will say, 'Yes.' You have validated your summary interpretation. Everything else was 'local color,' a natural part of story telling and narrative interaction, but not essential to describing the leasing option.

Interpreting what was essential, you left out certain elements. Later there might be a question like 'Who should we lease from?' and then 'LeaseCo' might be one of the options, but you don't need to try to get all that up front. If the group wants to explore the leasing option there will be a point when the whole group considers it together. Note that you don't need to direct the flow or facilitate the group to 'stay on topic' – the participants can see their whole discussion in the map, and they are best equipped to determine what issues need addressing and which can be left for later. And if you've left out an important point, it will come up again. This is all about the dance.

One of the services you are providing as a dialogue mapper is that you are crafting with the group a succinct summary of the logic and flow of the meeting conversation. If you wrote down everything that was said, your maps would amount to transcripts. For practical purposes summary maps are much more useful – and more likely to be read, understood, and circulated than a transcript.

Several years ago we facilitated a planning meeting for a group of high-ranking officers in the Marine Corps. As usual, a key product from that meeting was the dialogue map of the meeting discussion. At the beginning of the next meeting we presented the map to a general who had not been able to attend the first meeting. After studying the map for a few moments, he said, 'From everything I've heard from the people who were at that meeting, this map seems to capture the whole meeting. This is really amazing – after looking at this I feel like I was there!' Thus, an interpretive summary adds value – it is the sketch that shows the key details, not the photograph. Of course, a map's value depends on the level of ownership by the group that created it – validating the map with the group is the key to their ownership and buy-in.

Moreover, it is important to appreciate that you are *always* making interpretive choices. Even if you were videotaping the meeting, you would be making choices about when to start and stop the camera, where to point it, and who to zoom in on. So, there is no getting away from being interpretive – perfect transcription is impossible. The point is that you can't get away from being responsible for what is in the map – you are the primary author, even if it seems that you were just being transcriptive for the whole meeting.

As we noted above, you are making tons of choices when you are dialogue mapping: who to listen to if several people are talking, where you look and who you look at, what you say, what you write, when you validate, how you do the validation, what you do with the map at the breaks, and so on.

In another sense, there isn't really any choice at all. Dialogue mapping is meant to be like dancing with a partner. As you move, your partner immediately adjusts and moves. As they move, you adjust and move. Your movements don't occur as a set of options from which you select, you simply do what 'feels right' in each moment. Sometimes there is a sense of choosing your overall tone – will you be playful? Quiet? Serious? Enthusiastic? Again, these may seem like conscious choices, or they may seem like natural responses to your environment . . . just doing what feels right.

It is useful to be aware of the spectrum from transcriptive to interpretive as you are dialogue mapping, particularly as you start practicing with groups. But there is not a 'right' way to be – there is simply being appropriate to the group and their needs, as well as your own needs. Sometimes you have to concentrate on the rhythm and the steps, but real dancing happens when you let go and just dance.

Notes

1. Recall that Compendium nodes have a 'Detail' section where extended text can be captured (see for example Figure 3.7 on p. 76). One of the benefits of Compendium is that you can capture extended comments and key details or examples in a node's detail without cluttering the map. Indeed, one trick for capturing a rambling comment in Compendium is to open a new node and start typing in the detail. When you're done, you and the speaker can look at what you have captured, make corrections, and decide together on a good summary for the label, which then appears in the map.

2. Social complexity dictates that some meetings have very little to do with solving a problem or making a decision, regardless of what the agenda says – sometimes the social network needs to exercise itself in complex and mysterious ways. When you find yourself in one of these meetings, it may be appropriate to just sit back and enjoy the show!

Part III

6
Question Types

One of the wonderful benefits of knowing dialogue mapping is that over time you begin to see and hear the meta-patterns that occur over and over in conversations. The IBIS notation, in particular, exposes a deeper layer of conversational order that is normally not apparent. Not only do Questions generally lead to Ideas, which in turn suggest Pros and Cons, but also certain types of Question lead to other types of Question. When you have mapped enough conversations you begin to recognize that there are actually only a few basic map structures. To see these meta-patterns, however, you need to 'see' the types of Question as they arise in the conversation, and the ways in which they interconnect time after time.

It turns out that there are actually only about seven major types of Question.[1] If you examine hundreds of dialogue maps you'll begin to notice that 98% of the Questions in the maps cluster into these seven categories. Knowing these types makes hearing 'hidden Questions' much easier, because you can be actively listening in a meeting for the seven types. When you get a 'mystery comment' that doesn't seem to fit the map, you just need to dig deeper to discover what type of new Question has just been 'snuck' into the conversation.

The Question types also relate to each other in recurring ways. It's more of a general pattern, as in the way sand dunes are arranged in the desert, than a real map, like a map of a city. Seeing these larger patterns in dialogue maps takes some practical experience, and requires being fluent in the basic IBIS structure. That means knowing about Question types will be more useful to you as you practice and gain experience with IBIS. But it never hurts to be on the lookout for the Question types, because they will help you anticipate what might be coming next in the conversation and the map.

Deontic Questions

These are questions that ask, 'What should we do?' This is the question at the root of virtually all design and problem-solving conversations. The name deontic comes from the Greek *deon*, meaning that which is binding or necessary, and refers to issues that ask, 'Given such and such resources and constraints, what would be the best plan, the best course for us to follow?'

Examples of deontic questions include:

- What should we do about violence in schools?
- What should our strategic plan be?
- Which company should we merge with?
- Where should we locate our new office?
- Should we invest in new technology X?

Each question asks for an exploration about possible action, to be taken in the future, to bring about a more desirable state of affairs, i.e. a 'solution.' Each question mentions a problem domain . . . 'violence in schools,' 'strategic plan,' 'merge with another company,' etc. Usually a group will need more context than such a brief statement to have a coherent discussion about a topic, but this 'micro context' serves as a reminder of whatever background discussions and context setting have taken place.

Nine times out of ten, the root issue in a map for a group discussion will be a deontic question. The answers to this root deontic question will be broad answers that describe a general solution or approach, e.g. 'Increase security,' 'Offer creative after-school alternatives,' etc. For each option, there will be a natural, even inevitable, flow of the conversation into just how to implement it. For that, we have instrumental questions.

Instrumental Questions

Instrumental questions ask about the instrumentality – the means and methods – for achieving some objective. The general form is, 'How should we do it?' For example:

- How should we increase security?
- How should we implement this policy?
- How should we cut costs?
- What is the best way to increase sales?

While the deontic question asks *what* to do, the instrumental question asks *how* to do it.

Notice that instrumental questions invoke a linguistic frame in which, for the moment, it is assumed that X will be done, and now we want to explore *how* to do X. (In the next chapter we discuss the way to map the conversation when such an assumption is challenged.) Thus, if the board of directors has just decided to merge with ZipCo, Inc., the officers of the company may have a meeting in which the root issue is instrumental: 'How should we merge with ZipCo?'

If the root question isn't deontic, it is usually instrumental; these are the two core question types of any design or problem-solving process.

Criterial Questions

Another very important kind of question asks, 'What are the criteria?' This question is generally linked to the root deontic or instrumental question. It asks for the abstract requirements or goals. Examples include:

- What are the criteria for this decision?
- What are the goals on this project?
- What are the requirements?
- What do we need?
- Criteria?

In design terminology, criterial questions call for top down thinking, whereas deontic and instrumental questions call for bottom up think-

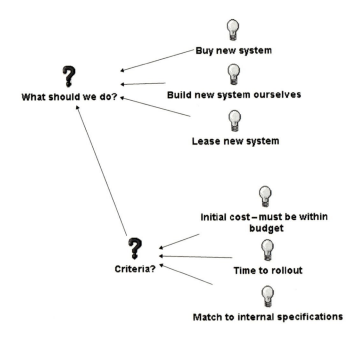

ing. Both are necessary. Methodologies that start with requirements will tell you to put the criterial questions on the agenda for a problem-solving session; it's OK to do that, but not necessary. Criterial questions will always come up spontaneously the moment a group is ready to start considering their problem from a more high-level or general perspective.

Meaning or Conceptual Questions

It is astounding how much time a group can spend arguing about an issue without stopping to make sure that everyone is talking about the same thing. Meaning questions arise frequently in dealing with wicked problems and social complexity. The general form of the meaning question is very simple: 'What does "X" mean?' Examples include:

- What does 'architecture' mean?
- What does 'empowering employees' mean?
- What does 'sticky web page' mean?
- What does 'terrorism' mean?

One way a dialogue mapper can add tremendous value to a difficult discussion is to ask the group a meaning question. The question usually seems silly. Several people will rush to explain the 'obvious' answer to the naïve dialogue mapper, and then find themselves vehemently disagreeing with each other.

Such cases often center on new terminology, especially in a technical area, but can be as simple as one faction thinking that 'short term' means 'less than a year' while the other faction thinks it means 'one or two months' (as once happened to us). The result in that case was a discussion on the deontic question, 'What should be our short-term plan?' that had more heat than light, and had devolved into a silly argument. At that point we raised the meaning question, 'What does "short term" mean?' Once the question had been captured and explored in the map, the participants could be more precise in their language, and they quickly got on with their planning exercise. The point with meaning questions is more to address the question collectively, exposing the range of meanings in the room, than to come up with the 'right' meaning.

Factual Questions

Another common source of wasted group energy is an argument over matters of fact. It is quite amazing the energy that intelligent people can put into arguing over a matter that could be quickly resolved by reference to an outside source. The general form of the factual question is, 'What is X?' or 'Is X true?' Examples include:

- What is the company policy on layoffs?
- What is in the current budget?
- What is the latest version of the system?
- Is X compatible with Y?

Factual questions are generally answerable by referring to a reference document or an accepted expert in the relevant domain. The wonderful thing about recognizing that an issue is factual is that the question can be captured in the map, and then an action item immediately connected to it for someone to do the research and get the answer. At that point, further discussion is probably frivolous.

Background Questions

Background questions ask for the context or background of the meeting or situation. The general form is, 'What is the background to this project?' Background questions aren't tricky to ask or to answer, and they are not always needed. But if you start mapping a group's discussion, and you can hear that they don't have enough shared context about what the problem is or why they are gathered, it can be very useful to introduce this question type, or identify it when it shows up organically. Examples include:

- What is the problem?
- What is our context?
- Why are we doing this project?

Note that the linguistic frame of this question type ('What is . . .') is factual – it sounds as if there *is* a specific background and it simply needs to be spelled out. In fact, more often this question allows the participants to tell stories about what they are concerned about, what the history of the project is, why it was important to have this meeting, and why this particular group is gathered together. In the process of telling these stories the group does essential work: creating shared meaning and context. If you capture these stories it adds a wonderful richness to the maps and the group memory.

Stakeholder Questions

The general form of this question type is, 'Who are the stakeholders of this project?' Other ways of getting at the stakeholders are:

- Who are the stakeholders?
- Whose buy-in is critical for our success?
- Who should the stakeholders be?
- Who cares about the outcome?

This question is especially powerful in situations of high social complexity. It is very likely that different individuals, or cliques, or factions, will have different notions of who the stakeholders are. (See the discussion of stakeholders and social complexity in Chapter 1.) Asking this question leads the group to collectively consider whose ownership or buy-in is crucial to the decision they are about to make, which in turn can surface new criteria, new ideas, new arguments, and new issues. The power of this question type is revealed by the peril of ignoring it: any project that fails to take account of a key stakeholder, whether deliberately or by accident, creates the certainty of a bumpy road ahead, and the real possibility of complete project failure. An inventory of stakeholders allows you to determine your strategy for each stakeholder . . . even if the strategy is 'do nothing.' The peril is in not having considered your strategy.

The Meta-Map

Now that we have reviewed the question types we can take a peek at the geometry of the dialog meta-map – a pattern of timing and structural relationships among the question types that helps the dialogue mapper see what is coming next and where to put it in the map.

Figure 6.1 shows a rendering of this meta-map. The root Question (1.) is the generic deontic question, 'What should we do?' There are

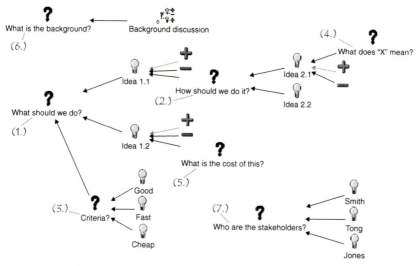

Figure 6.1   Dialogue mapping meta-map

two responding Ideas, each with some Pros and Cons. In this case, the first Idea has an instrumental Question (2.) expanding on it, and the second Idea has a factual Question (5.) that expands on it. Evidently the technical term 'X' is used in Idea 2.1, because there is a meaning Question (4.) probing for a definition. At some point in the discussion there's a review of the background (6.), which has been put into the sub-map 'Background discussion.' The criterial Question (3.), simply 'Criteria?', is attached to the root Question. Finally, the stakeholder Question (7.) is 'floating' in the lower right of the map.

This map suggests the general layout and flow of most design and problem-solving conversations. By convention, dialogue maps grow from left to right and top to bottom, but new questions are sometimes put higher or to the left in the map if they are considered logically or temporally 'prior' to the existing root. Thus, the meta-map in Figure 7.1 represents a highly simplified template of a *mature* dialogue map – a map for a given meeting might start with any one of these questions, and grow in all directions.

Don't bother with memorizing this map – with practice you will develop your own meta-map that reflects your style of phrasing questions and laying them out in maps.

Artful Questions

Although not a question type exactly, there is an aesthetic to IBIS Questions that is both a challenge and an opportunity for dialogue mapping, and it is worth touching on here.

Artful questions must be simple, not compound. 'What are they planning, and how are they going to do it?' is a compound question – in IBIS it should be broken into its two component questions.

Artful questions do not try to 'sneak' major assumptions into their statement, e.g. 'Why don't we hire any competent administrators around here?'

And artful questions are open, not closed. 'What should we do?' is open, 'Should we cut costs?' is closed.

A closed question is one for which the answer is 'yes' or 'no,' or which lists the possible answers in the question (e.g. 'Should we cut costs or raise our prices?'). Closed questions offer a choice among given options. Closed questions seem to 'stack the deck' and close the mind to new possibilities. Years of experience have shown that IBIS discussions that start with open questions are more creative and rigorous.

Fortunately, it is easy to 'open' a closed question. Suppose the starting question is 'Should we cut costs?' To open the question, simply locate the answer buried inside the question (in this case, 'cut costs') and restate the simplified question with the answer as an Idea: 'What should we do?,' 'Cut costs' (see Figure 6.2). All of the analysis about the option to cut costs can then be attached to the idea, 'Cut costs.'

Figure 6.2   Opening up a question in IBIS
Note: The forms are logically equivalent: the same arguments, issues, and evidence that apply to 'Yes' on the left apply to 'Cut costs' on the right

As it happens, everyday speech uses more closed questions than open ones, and so do most meeting agendas. Occasionally, dialogue mappers are called on by their clients to facilitate discussions on closed questions. The challenge is this: Closed yes/no questions are so rooted in our culture and our everyday way of speaking that it may be easier to accept the closed question and work with it, at least initially. Let the group have a discussion on the Pros and Cons of 'yes' and 'no',[2] even though you know it's just a matter of time before someone says, 'Well, what if we increased prices instead?,' thus offering an option that can't be connected to the yes/no question. At that point you can let the group help you open the Question up. Remove the embedded idea and post it as its own Idea node (as in Figure 6.2), restate the Question in open form . . . and bask in the gratitude of a group that just got pulled out of a common discussion rut.

Map as Mirror

Knowing the Question types and the meta-map may help clarify how the dialogue map acts as a sort of 'mirror' in which the group can see itself more clearly, especially its behavior. Disruptive behavior patterns show up rather obviously. If a participant goes off topic with a comment, the dialogue mapper can work with him or her to find out how to capture the comment either as a new question or as a node linked to an existing part of the map; either way, the topic shift shows up clearly in the geometry of the map. If a participant challenges the whole frame of the meeting (e.g. 'Why are we talking about this? This isn't the real issue!') the dialogue mapper can capture that comment in a clear way – a 'left-hand move' – that captures the participant's concern and any discussion about it without undermining the rest of the meeting's discussion (see next chapter). If someone asks a closed question (e.g. 'Should we abandon that product line?'), the yes/no options in the map reflect the limiting frame of the question. Thus the dialogue map allows the group to see the conversational patterns it uses, perhaps with your help, and supports the participants in upgrading those patterns into more productive ones quite naturally.

The Criterial Leap

How do you know if you have listed all of the criteria on a criterial Question? How can you check to see if there are any important arguments (Pro or Con) missing from the map? There is a technique for this, and it's called the 'criterial leap.' To understand how it works, first consider the example in Figure 6.3 showing a simple deontic Question with a few Ideas and Arguments. This is an early snapshot of the map a group might come up with that was considering what their organization should do to replace an aging software system.

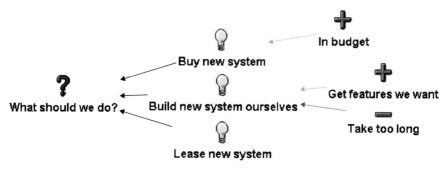

Figure 6.3 A simple deontic Question with Ideas and Arguments

At some point in the discussion, someone might say something like, 'No matter what we do, our initial cost for this replacement system project has to be within the budget we've been given.' You might at first think this move is a new argument, but it isn't. The clue is the phrase, 'No matter what we do.' In other words, *any* solution (any possible Idea on the Question) will be subject to this criterion. This statement, then, is the signal that it's time for a criterial Question in the map, as shown in Figure 6.4.

The criterial Question provides a place, a sort of 'bucket,' for all the criteria as they arise in the conversation to be captured as 'criterial Ideas.' It takes some practice to spot them, but the key is that criteria apply to *any possible* Idea/solution on the main Question.

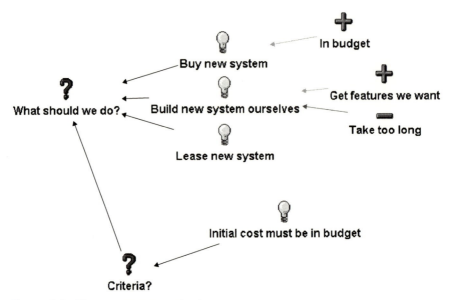

Figure 6.4   How to capture a criterion

Now we can talk about the criterial leap: inspect Figure 6.4 for a moment and find all of the nodes that have to do with cost. See the connection? There is an association between the argument 'In budget' and the criterion 'Initial cost must be in budget.' These two nodes are *not* saying the same thing! The criterion about the budget is higher level – it is a general statement about all possible solutions. 'In budget,' the Pro on 'Buy a new system,' is a specific argument that *that particular option* is within the budget. The invisible connection between these two nodes is a *criterial leap*.

One way to check on the completeness of a dialogue map as it matures is the correspondence between the criterial Ideas and the deontic (or instrumental) Pros and Cons. They are at different levels, but they inform each other. If 'Get features we want' is an important argument, at *some point* it should show up as a criterion on the criterial Question. Thus, in this example it is likely that at a more mature phase this map will look like Figure 6.5, in which the arguments correspond with the criteria. It is important to note that dialogue mapping has nothing to say about whether you start with the criteria (top down thinking) or the arguments on the options (bottom up thinking) – the map flows just as easily whichever part gets developed first.

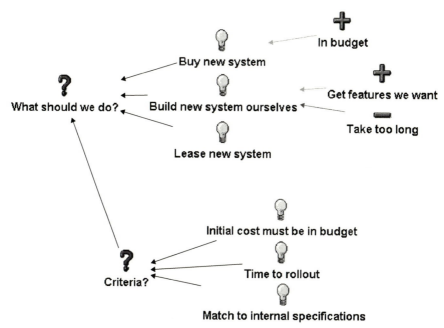

Figure 6.5 Mature map with criterion for every argument

The criterial leap is not about making sure that there's a complete correspondence between criterial Ideas and deontic Pros and Cons – it is about having a way, as a map or discussion is drawing toward closure, to make sure that everything that needs to be said about criteria and pros and cons has been said (see also Chapter 9 on decision making).

Factual Questions in Political Contexts

In Chapter 1 we talked about the fundamental tension inherent in any design conversation between people representing the engineering/technology side (what-can-be-done) and the sales/marketing side (what-is-needed). One aspect of that tension that bears noting in this chapter on Question types is the different notions of truth or validity in these two domains.[3] For the engineer, facts are facts. Facts have an objectively verifiable validity. For the engineer, a factual Question is straightforward: it is asking to have the one right and true answer plugged into it. It would be silly for there to be Pros and Cons about that Idea.

For the marketer, or indeed in any realm that deals with social systems, and especially politics, truth and validity are a lot more flexible. It's not that you can make anything up and say it's true, but there's a lot more room for contextual differences, for interpretation, and for partial validity. For the marketer a factual Question can have multiple valid or partly valid answers, each with its own qualification.

Where conversations can get in trouble – and where dialogue mappers need to stay particularly alert – is when the topic lies between these two realms. My favorite example is the simple factual question, 'What is the Pashtun population of Afghanistan?' On the face of it, the answer is a number, a population figure or estimate. It doesn't have to be precise, but the question appears to be an engineering-realm kind of question. Neither is it an idle question: the design of a representative government for Afghanistan, for example, rests on the relative populations of its various ethnic groups.

The best answer to this question, however, turns out to be, 'It depends where you draw the borders between Afghanistan and its neighbors.' The southern border between Afghanistan and Pakistan is, in particular, a matter of historical debate.[4] Moreover, in a political context there are *lots* of questions of this type; relative truth questions masquerading as objective truth questions. Indeed, this is a hallmark of wicked problems and social complexity. Politics is not restricted to government organizations – a system development project in a high-tech company can be *highly* political!

Such questions lure groups into having heated and strident debate over the 'right' answer, each speaker certain that his or her 'objectively verifiable' answer is the correct one. Dialogue mapping the discussion can be tricky, because the very existence of a map showing multiple answers to such a question threatens each participant's belief that his or her 'truth' is absolute and obvious, the others wrong and dangerous. This context of infallibility is even more shaken if the dialogue mapper encourages the participants to make cases for their answer, i.e. to offer Pros and Cons.

In any case the group will be best served by having this kind of debate mapped, so that the arguments and claims are exposed to the harsh light of the group's rational intelligence. On one such occasion I called a break when the discussion stalled, so that the resolution of the debate could happen in the hallway, offline and off the meeting discussion stage. After the break we captured the resolution in the map.

Notes

1. The typology of questions described here is inspired by Horst Rittel's early work, especially as reported in Kunz and Rittel, 1970, but expands it based on our experience in the decades since.
2. Pros and Cons of yes and no can get ugly and confusing. Either put up just the Idea 'yes', and capture the Pros and Cons to it, or put up both 'yes' and 'no' and capture all arguments as Pros (Cons for no get turned into Pros for yes, and vice versa).
3. For a nice discussion of different realms of truth and validity, see Chapter 6 in Wilbur, 1996.
4. One version of the border, for example, is the Durand Line, named after the British official who oversaw the demarcation of the 19th-century boundary; but it has never been officially ratified.

7
Three Moves of Discourse

Think of a meeting as a game. There are players, rules, moves, structure, winners, and losers. Like chess or checkers, only with more players, and a lot more chaos. There may be teams, or it may be each participant for him- or herself. Sometimes players can switch teams, or be on several teams at once – the rules aren't very clear. Each time someone speaks, it is a move in the game. Players make moves to win the game, but – again – the rules are a bit vague on how you win and what it looks like. Indeed, it is not unusual for different players to have different rules with different definitions of winning.

But if you have played enough of the meeting discourse game, there are some moves that you recognize immediately. This chapter is about three very common kinds of moves that are problematic in meetings because they are powerful moves that some people regard as cheating. These three moves require everyone to sit up and pay attention. They can upset the balance of power in the room, and invoke strong feelings among the players. The three moves are:

1 Making a case *for* an idea or proposal.
2 Making a case *against* an idea or proposal.
3 Challenging the *context*/frame of the conversation.

As we review these three kinds of move, it is important to observe the crazy-making dichotomy in which these moves are held. On the one hand, each move expresses an energy or intention that is essential to creative problem solving – any healthy team or project would want to make sure that all three of these kinds of energy were present.

On the other hand, each move has a stigma associated with it. If you are someone who makes these moves very often, it could damage your reputation. You might find yourself sitting alone in the company cafeteria. At the end of the day, it makes us collectively crazy that we recognize that these moves are essential to the problem-solving process, and at the same time we shun the moves and the players who make them.

As we'll see below, dialogue mapping has the power to take the sting out of these moves, because it becomes clear that the moves aren't *personal*. The moves get made and captured, the energy behind them is contributed to the project, and the process of thinking and learning about the wicked problem rolls on. No one needs to take the moves personally, or to change how they participate. Powerful moves are not a problem because the container for the meeting discourse is strong enough to hold them. The group stays focused on the project, not on personalities.

Making a Case for an Idea

We've all had the experience of being in a meeting when someone starts making a really strong case for something he wants. He offers reasons why it's the right thing to do, and strongly suggests, either directly or by innuendo, that things will go much better if the group backs his option . . . and really bad things will happen if the group doesn't. He finds ways to work his idea into other topics throughout the meeting, so that it seems that all decisions will be made easier if his idea gets selected. This is case making, and we may find ourselves thinking uncharitably of the guy who does it . . . as a zealot or a monomaniac.

By way of contrast, imagine that you are at a meeting, and a topic you know a lot about comes up, and you *know* in your heart of hearts what the right thing to do is. You have a lot of experience with the situation, you've studied the data, you've thought about it a lot – it seems pretty obvious to you. Sure, other people have a right to their opinions, but your solution, it seems to you, is *far* superior to the other options being considered.

If you are serious about having your idea considered you will need to make a case for it – you'll need to explain the merits and benefits of your proposal, and you might need to defend your idea from criticisms by other players. One of the few clear big wins of the meeting game is for a player or team to move a new idea from initial proposal all the way to the endgame of being adopted by the group as the official solution to the problem. Your ability to make such a winning move depends critically on your willingness to speak clearly and compellingly for a proposal – to make a case for it.

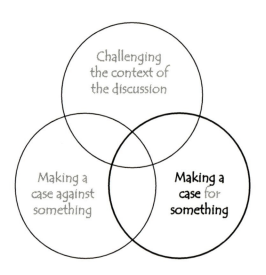

But there are corporate cultures in which it is considered bad form to make a strong case for an idea. Especially in a bureaucracy, it is considered naïve or pushy and perhaps egotistical to put an idea on the table and really make a strong case for it. If the stigma of case making isn't cultural, it may be personal – you may work with someone who, when they speak up for something, causes you to roll your eyes and think, 'Oh, here we go again!' You may not even disagree with their point of view, but you are expecting the case making to be repetitive and painful.

Let us say you are in a meeting about the company's vacation policy – Ed Smith, the Vice President, wants to eliminate the option to carry over unused vacation days to the following year as part of a new cost-cutting program:

We had a guy earlier this year who took *9 weeks* of vacation he had accrued, all at once! It really messed up his department! People need to understand that vacation time is a limited benefit – use it or lose it! Heaven forbid all these vacation savers all take off at once – work will grind to a halt around here. We need to just put an end to the carry over option. People are abusing it, and it's costing us a lot of money.

His points may be valid or not. They may or may not be compelling. But Ed Smith is clearly intent on getting the vacation policy changed, and he is outspoken about his case for it. At this point groups usually do one of several things: succumb to the dominant player, sit quietly looking at their pencils or the floor, or start picking the arguments apart. In any case, the group has a problem: how to deal with Ed.

Dialogue mapping can take the sting out of this situation. You simply capture the Idea being promoted and the Pros for it – you map the case. You recognize that the energy behind the case making – a forward-moving, let's-get-going, let's-make-a-decision energy – is valuable energy, and you exploit that energy by capturing the case. The case making, far from being a problem the group has to stop and handle, becomes a contribution. It's a contribution because that forward-moving energy, channeled, is what makes results happen. You might even encourage it . . . 'These arguments are great! Do you have any other support for this idea? Does anybody else?'

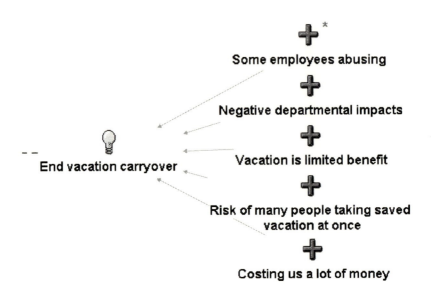

Instead of the player with the proposal feeling squelched or ignored, he or she experiences getting to make their contribution and being heard and acknowledged.

Remember, with collaborative display there is no incentive to repeat a point. Once the case has been made and captured, if the 'zealot' goes back to his or her proposal, the dialogue mapper can simply point to the Idea in the map and say 'Oh, are you talking about this proposal? Is there anything new that you want to add?' Truth by repetition is not a powerful move in the dialogue mapping game.

The forward-pushing energy of case making is essential to problem solving, and it can add velocity, momentum, and the joy of accomplishment to a project. The tendency to ostracize the person who is making a case is due simply to the lack of a rich enough container for that kind of energy in a meeting. Dialogue mapping provides that container. There is no problem with case making, it simply grows the map in a certain way, and when the case is made, it is captured. The only reason to revisit it will be to develop the idea further, learning about new facets of it.

Successful projects exploit all the different kinds of energy that people bring to the party, and capture the fruits of that energy as collective intelligence and learning. Without a shared display, you just don't have a rich enough container for all the kinds of energy that are happening, and people resort to trying to change or suppress each other to deal with all of that creative energy. With the shared display, the container holds and nurtures the diverse energies that people bring to project meetings.

Once you know that case making is not inherently a problem, just an expression of an important kind of energy, it helps you relax and trust yourself and the dialogue mapping process. It helps you remember that you are reflecting the group's energy and moves back to itself, so that the participants can learn, grow, and self-correct. You come to trust the group's process instead of trying to control it.

Making a Case against an Idea

Most of us prefer harmony to discord. We prefer agreement and consensus to rancor and debate. With a tame problem, a well-oiled team can often maintain a very agreeable atmosphere. But wicked problems introduce high levels of uncertainty, an overload of information, and changing roles and circumstances. These factors increase social tension, and there is more disagreement, within both the team and the larger social network, about what is needed, what we should do, who we are, and where we are going. In these settings, a common creativity-killing move in meetings tries to shoot down a proposal or idea . . . 'it won't work,' 'it's too expensive,' 'we tried it before,' 'it will take too long,' and so on.

Imagine that you are in the meeting above, Ed Smith has made his proposal, and Cheryl Green, VP of HR, says, 'I don't think that will work, Ed. First, vacation time is like any other benefit, it doesn't expire. Second, the people you affect by dropping vacation carry over are our most senior and loyal employees. And third, dropping it may not be legal in this state.' As the two opponents face off for debate, you can feel that maybe this isn't just about the vacation policy – this is about who will be the victor in this skirmish.

Without dialogue mapping in a shared display, case making against an idea is 'being negative.' It is bringing up problems and barriers and objections, and the person who does it is often viewed as being cynical, difficult, negative, or not a 'team player.'

Just as with making a case for an idea, dialogue mapping shifts the dynamics of case making against an idea. First, when the idea is pre-

sented, it gets captured in the display. It now has a place in the room
other than the person who suggested it! This is a wonderful 'trick'
of collaborative display: simply creating a physical separation
between the person who proposed the idea and the idea itself (see
Figure 7.1). It lessens the tendency to be identified with one's point
of view, or to be defensive about any criticism of it.

Figure 7.1 Physical separation between proposer of idea and the idea itself

Arguments for and against the idea (Pros and Cons) also have a place
in the room: up in the display, next to the idea. It is safer to make a
case against an idea because it isn't an attack on the person who suggested it, the case is simply some 'minus' icons with arrows pointing at the idea. In fact, the dialogue mapper can encourage the case
making against the idea, pointing to it and saying, 'We have plenty
of pros for this idea . . . are there any cons?'

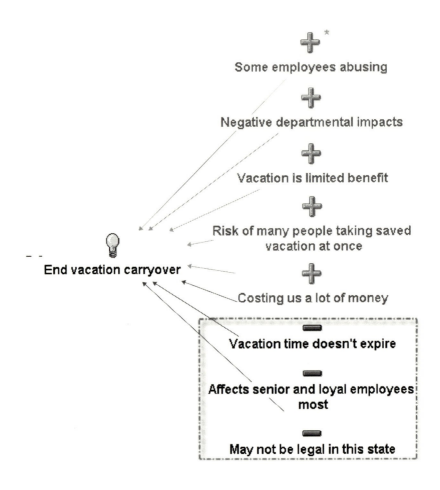

With dialogue mapping, there is more room to express doubt and objections to a proposal. More room for a very important kind of energy: the energy of prudence, restraint, and diligence. As important as the forward-pushing energy of positive case making is, it is also essential to have the energy of prudence and restraint in a project. Colossal mistakes have been avoided because someone had the courage to speak up and voice an objection that no one else knew about or had thought of.

Dialogue mapping holds this energy in a container that allows it to make its contribution without being toxic. It says, 'We need to know the objections to an idea before we adopt it, because we're bound to hear them eventually. Also, overlooked objections could cause the project to fail, so we had better understand potential problems *now* before we make the decision. We value the critical thinking that will help us come up with the best possible solution.'

As a map unfolds and matures, the Cons to key Ideas require careful attention. Each such Con requires that either:

- The Con is 'retired,' by further discussion showing that it isn't valid.[1]
- The Idea is revised so that the Con no longer applies to it.
- Or the group decides that the Con is an acceptable objection or risk.

Dialogue mapping makes it safe and appropriate to surface these essential objections as a natural part of the problem solving or design process.

Challenging the Frame of the Discussion

This third move is sometimes called 'grenade throwing,' because of the impact it can have on a meeting discussion. Often this move is made by someone who has not been fully participating in the meeting. At some point he or she gets the floor and says something like, 'Why are we talking about this? This isn't the real issue!' This move is unlike the first two moves, in that it challenges the root *Question* . . . the frame in which the whole discussion is occurring.

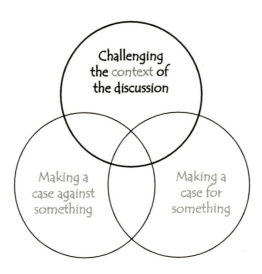

Here's an example: I was dialogue mapping a meeting for a group in the research division of a large cookie company. Part of the agenda for the meeting was to come up with ways to cut costs within the division. I started the group brainstorming on the Question, 'How to cut costs?' and the group quickly got into the game. Many people were coming up with ideas, and we were capturing them in the map (as Ideas, of course).

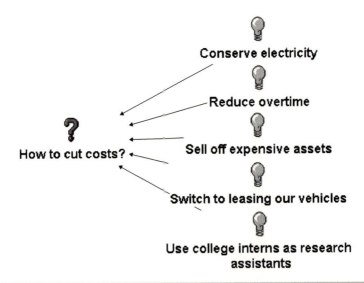

After a while there was a pause, as often happens during brain-storming, and a man named Jack at one corner of the conference room table almost spat out, 'Why are we talking about this? Aren't we a cookie company? Isn't the whole point around here to sell cookies? Why aren't we talking about *how to sell more cookies*?!?'

This was a defining moment for our fledgling dialogue mapping facil-itation service. You could hear a pin drop in the room, and you got the feeling that this might not be the very first time Jack had made this kind of move in a meeting. All eyes turned toward me. 'How will he deal with this grenade?' was the silent question in the room.

Without saying a word, I made some space under the first question and typed in the new Question, 'How to sell more cookies?'

'Is this the question you're asking?'

'Yes, it is,' the man said.

'And, do you have any ideas about it?' I asked.

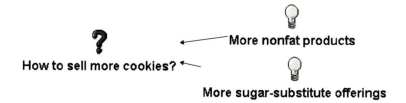

'As a matter of fact, I do,' he said, and he described his idea, which I captured in the map. Then I asked the group, 'Does anyone else have any ideas on this one?', pointing to the Question in the display. One person raised her hand and I captured her idea.

Then someone else said, 'I have another idea about cutting costs.' I scrolled the display up so you could see all of the cost-cutting ideas and said, 'Shoot.' And the group went back to their brainstorming session about cost-cutting measures.

In short, the grenade didn't go off . . . there was no grenade. There was just someone who needed to have a larger frame for the discussion in order to participate. The root question of the map wasn't *his* root question.

The power of collaborative display is that there is no scarcity of room to consider *lots* of Questions. Indeed, if a problem is wicked and/or if the social complexity quotient is high, there will be many, many Questions that the group cares about. Absent a collaborative display, the facilitator has to focus the group on just one or two of these questions. The group has to suppress the rest, or if they come up they get sent to the 'parking lot.' Remember the description of opportunity-driven problem solving from Chapter 1 . . . the jagged line that bounced chaotically from problem understanding to solution and back? When the problem is wicked, a group needs a container that allows their collective thinking and learning process to bounce around like that, among several Questions, even several different topics at times.

Dialogue mapping provides this kind of container by making it easy to simply add a new Question, often parallel to and below the preceding Question(s). Then the group can explore that question as long as they need to. There is no risk, by the way, that the group will get lost on this 'sidetrack' – the display makes it vividly clear that the preceding question is still sitting there, waiting to be returned to. The dialogue mapper usually does not even have to say anything to bring them back – the group knows the original question is there, waiting,

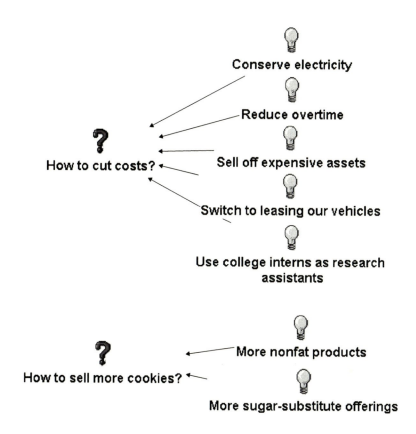

and they know (once they've learned to trust the display) when they're ready to go back to it.

Our story doesn't quite end there, however. Just before the end of the meeting, I pointed out to Jack that the whole group had actually been addressing the same concern all along. He just looked at me, so I started typing and talking.

'The question we started with, "How to cut costs?," was about the basic idea, "Cut costs." Similarly, your question was about the idea, "Sell more cookies." Now, look at the map for a moment . . . what new question are both of these ideas addressing?'

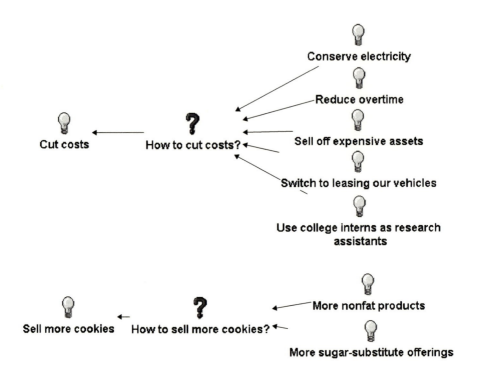

Jack saw it right away. 'How to increase profit, right?'

'That's what I think,' I said as I created the new Question. The two separate Questions from the meeting suddenly were clearly aspects of the same larger Question.

'Wow,' a woman said laughing, 'and I thought Jack was just trying to get us off track again!'

This move, creating a new root Question, turns out to be one of the most powerful tools in the dialogue mapper's toolkit. It even has a special name: the *left-hand move,* because it has the effect of moving the beginning of the map to the left. The left-hand move provides a powerful device for maintaining coherence when a group or someone

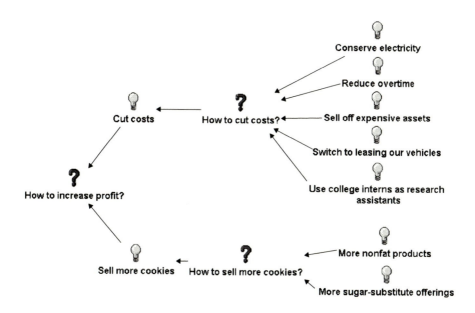

in it does not accept the framing assumptions of the current conversation. Instead of blowing up the discussion and putting everyone on edge, it simply acknowledges that one of the assumptions in the background of the project or the meeting just got surfaced, and needs to be acknowledged.

It's important to note that making a left-hand move does not force you or the group to actually discuss the new root Question. Often it is enough to simply note that it's there. In one meeting, at a large software company, the group needed to spend just a couple of minutes figuring out how to state the new root Question, and then assigning someone to take it to management after the meeting and find out what their input was.

To summarize, when someone challenges the frame of the discussion, it calls for either a new parallel Question or a new root Question. In either case, the 'philosopher's' disruption is minimal, and indeed often reflects the energy of making sure we're having the right conversation, at the right level.

Note

1. An Idea can be marked as retired by wrapping its label in parentheses, e.g. '(End vacation carryover)'. This indicates that it is no longer under consideration. In general you should retire only Ideas that *no one* supports.

8
Limits of Dialogue Mapping

There are situations where dialogue mapping works really well, and situations where it doesn't work at all. As with any structure for human interaction, these situations cannot be tightly defined or delimited, but there are some broad patterns that are useful to understand.

When Corporate Memory Systems, Inc., of which I was a co-founder, was first starting up in the early 1990s, our marketing and fund-raising plan featured a very simple idea. We would sell our QuestMap software and consulting and training services to electric utility companies, because they needed to improve their corporate memories. There were many examples of electric utilities that had been penalized millions of dollars by their state's regulatory commission because the utility could not explain decisions they had made years before. Why they had decided to build a certain nuclear power plant, for example, or why they bought coal at a certain price. Using 20-20 hindsight, the prudence of past decisions was often challenged, but usually the utility executives had no basis for justifying those decisions they had made years before.

That marketing strategy – selling corporate memory to utilities – failed, and Corporate Memory Systems, Inc. went out of business several years later. There were many reasons, but chief among them was that it turned out that utility company executives did not want to go on record for their decision-making process or rationale. Evidently, it was worth millions of dollars in fines to be able to continue making mission-critical, high-stakes decisions the old-fashioned way: behind closed doors.

As entrepreneurs we were flabbergasted. Could it be that it was somehow *worth* the risk of those huge penalties to keep making decisions in secret, without documentation? By contrast, in our little fledgling company of about eight employees, we operated in a very open and democratic way. We celebrated that the only secret in the company was employee salaries. The executive team made the big decisions, of course, but we were at pains to sit down with the staff and include them as much as possible. And virtually all of our corporate planning and decision making was conducted in QuestMap[1], where everyone could see it, and dialogue mapping was a routine part of many company meetings. But not all of them.

In the limit, dialogue mapping is just a tool . . . a technique for group communication. The emphasis should really be on the *dialogue mapper*, for it is the listening skills, the mapping skills, and the intention to be of service that really defines the power – and the limits – of dialogue mapping.

There is subtlety that experienced facilitators revel in when they learn dialogue mapping – that you can stop trying to be brilliant and *trust* the group and the display. You don't need to deal with difficult personalities or lead the group out of debate – just trust IBIS (find the hidden question), trust the listening cycle (honor individuals to honor the group), and trust the group's natural intelligence.

In this chapter we will explore the social limitations of dialogue mapping – some real, some imagined – and how to deal with those limitations and concerns. (There are also some limitations of dialogue mapping that are not social but technical or methodological. For example, there are situations where the best structure for a group collaboration is a matrix, or a large calendar, or a system dynamics model, etc. These are times to use dialogue mapping *and* other techniques, methods, and notations.) In the end, the point of this chapter is to better equip you, the dialogue mapper, to recognize when to turn on the display and get mapping, and when to turn it off and just be with the group.

Democracy versus Politics

One of the chief features of dialogue mapping is that the process strongly reflects *democratic values*, such as being open, transparent, accountable, honest, and fair. This is not to say that it only works in a democracy, i.e. where the decision-making process is by majority vote. Dialogue mapping is a great way to formulate a recommendation to an executive, which he or she may or may not accept. But dialogue mapping inherently fosters a democratic spirit of equality and openness among its participants. Conversely, a group often needs to value these qualities to even be drawn to using dialogue mapping.

There are work environments in which equality and openness are not highly valued. For example, dialogue mapping sessions have sometimes failed in highly 'political' environments, where participants are not necessarily saying everything they know, and mutually constructive dialogue is less important than power plays.[2] This track record goes back to the earliest experiences with IBIS. Horst Rittel, the inventor of the IBIS approach, got the German Parliament to experiment with using it in the 1970s (Rittel, personal communication). The politicians liked the document management aspects of his system, but after a while insisted he stop capturing and structuring their discussions in IBIS. Evidently, it just recorded too much of the wrong kinds of details. Similarly, I once dialogue mapped a session for a legislative group in the US Congress – they paid little attention to the display, and asked that the dialogue map database be destroyed at the end of the session.

It would be tempting to cast work environments along a spectrum from open/democratic to political/totalitarian. Open/democratic settings would be open and apolitical, actively pursuing democratic values and eschewing power struggles. Such a characterization would obscure an important point, however. Power relations are fundamental to human social interaction, and the real lines of influence, control, and power are always obscure, usually deliberately. Some level of power struggle and hidden control is a natural part of human social systems, including democracy. It is a matter of degree, and – most importantly – a matter of what the organization or group is committed to.

Dialogue mapping is democratic because it creates a level playing field among the participants – each participant's point of view is captured and displayed equally. Normally, when an authority figure speaks and makes a case for his or her idea, the group tends to authorize that point of view – to give it added weight and validity, simply because of who is advocating it or how they are saying it. Once that case is displayed in the map, however, there is a degree of separation between advocate and case, and it must stand on its own. If the logic is weak or biased, it will be more obvious in the map than it was under the spell of a charismatic presentation. Similarly, if there is another case in the map, made perhaps by the most junior person in the room, if the logic is clear and compelling, that too will stand out in the map, and that idea will have more real authority. To the extent that the facilitated shared display is the medium of the conversation, authority tends to shift from personalities to the merits of the case.

This has led to a few cases where a senior leader in a client meeting asked for the dialogue mapping display to be turned off, and other cases where dialogue mapping facilitation, although popular and successful with the group, was only tried once.

Transparency of Rationale and Process

Why would a leader want to turn off dialogue mapping? What are his or her concerns?

To explore this issue, let's first take a step back and review how a case gets made in a dialogue map. There are three structural elements that make a case compelling:

1 There are strong supporting arguments for the idea. 'Cheapest option,' 'Exactly what the customer is asking for' . . . these are strong arguments. Strong arguments are those that appeal to the key criteria for the issue, such as cost, quality, and speed.
2 Any strong objecting arguments have been retired, or the Idea revised to address the objections. If there is an argument, 'Too expensive, $100K over budget,' then there would be a challenging Question such as 'How to do it within budget?' that links to viable Ideas for cutting costs.

3   Critical instrumental, meaning, and factual Questions have been answered in an informed and thorough way. A proposal will be more compelling if the group has thought through its implementation and understands the hidden complexities and consequences that might appear.

Thus there is a 'geometry of case quality' in a dialogue map – you can tell by inspecting the map where the most thought and rigor has been invested.

I claim that these qualities of clarity and transparency of rationale and process promote project success because they foster the highest levels of shared understanding, ownership, and commitment from the group. The patterns of case making in the map will be a strong indicator of the quality of that ownership. Of course, the map will never tell the whole story. The map is simply an artifact of the group's exploration of a complex set of ideas embedded in a rich cultural, political, and interpersonal context. The map is a kind of story. It will mean very different things to insiders than to outsiders. Nonetheless, because the rationale for an idea or decision is embedded in it, a dialogue map can be a compelling artifact of group thinking.

Thus, the process of crafting a map with a dialogue mapper's guidance tends to be democratic and transparent. The intent of dialogue mapping is an open dialogue among stakeholders oriented to getting all points of view expressed and captured and all relevant information linked in. All ideas are allowed and considered, regardless of the source. All questions are legitimate. All arguments are considered. Power is not represented in the shared display. For example, Ideas are not attributed to a speaker, neither is a participant's title reflected in the graphics of the map. I may be backing a certain proposal as a 'political favor' to a colleague, but it is still incumbent on me to make a case for the proposal that stands up to logical scrutiny.

Of course, using dialogue mapping does not impose a democratic process. You could have one Idea with 16 Pro arguments supporting it, and right below it another Idea with a single Pro argument: 'The General insists on this.' It is clear what the decision will be, and it is clear that power, not argumentation, made the decision. This does not make it irrational – it is simply the rationality of a hierarchical decision-making process. What may be different with dialogue mapping is that, whatever the rationality, the logic is transparent. It is not cloaked in rhetoric or hidden in closed-door sessions. It is explicit. If the General is willing to go on record as overriding the group's reasoning, then dialogue mapping can work fine in that situation.

While politics is an ordinary part of the social network, some organizations are mired in a highly politicized backfield of hidden agendas, cliques, and veiled manipulation. This environment thrives on secrets, closed meetings, misuse of authority, and opaque decisions. But no leader would advocate this kind of organizational culture, for no other reason than how inefficient it is at producing value for customers. Yet if there is an espoused commitment to democratic ideals, or to being a learning organization, openness and transparency must become real and operational, and that is strong medicine. Leadership can espouse a commitment to transparency and learning, but fail to see how they participate in undermining these values in seemingly 'minor' ways.

Chris Argyris has written in depth about 'skilled incompetence' (Argyris and Schön, 1996). In an organization where certain key topics and issues are 'undiscussable,' leaders and subordinates skillfully collude in subtle ways to avoid open discussion and learning. More management energy goes into working around the undiscussable topics than into leading the organization creatively. Senior leaders who have climbed to the top of the corporate ladder using high levels of skilled incompetence are scarcely going to embrace meeting facilitation techniques that expose the dynamics of influence and control. These are people whose own influence relies on charisma, relationships, and a facility with creating the propaganda that advances their cause and position. These leaders will not welcome dialogue mapping, and they will usually seek to ignore it and turn it off as quickly as possible, because it undermines their basis of power.

As the shift to a knowledge economy unfolds, more and more organizations are embracing practices and values consistent with learning, innovation, and providing a productive environment for knowledge workers. Knowledge workers on a wicked problem project team know that there can be no central authority because no single person knows all the information or the right answer. Moreover, knowledge work by definition deals with novel situations. Knowledge work, by its very nature, demands a transparent and democratic environment to grow and flourish.

Dialogue mapping can support the transition to more democratic processes, but only if there is a commitment to making that change.[3] When a leader uses a pro-democratic process like dialogue mapping, she sends a signal that is stronger than words, and more effective than seminars on communication and teamwork. She is walking the talk, using a technique that clearly values listening, honors clear and creative speaking, and makes the decision-making process transparent. Thus dialogue mapping can be a tool for a transition to a culture of transparency and learning. By the same token, absent this pro-democratic commitment, dialogue mapping can be rejected just as if it were a non-matching tissue type.

Is Dialogue Mapping Hyper-Rational?

All of this talk about logic and rationality can raise another concern: that using computers to map conversations deprives participants of the soul of their communication, that Post-its® and easel sheets are low-tech and natural, and that bringing a computer into the meeting context draws away the human element. Does using dialogue mapping imply a hyper-rational process that is leached of its humanity, and that strips away ambiguity and destroys nuances?

No, not inherently. The dialogue map tends to allow participants to be more objective about issues, and more conscious about their subjectivity. Most of what happens in a dialogue-mapped meeting is still a rich, multilayered, and mysterious process of human interaction. The presence of a shared display map can reduce the impact of dysfunctional behavior patterns, but it does not eliminate the emotional and nonverbal relating that naturally happens within a group. A skilled dialogue mapper can lead a group to true collective creativity and intelligence. Human process is and should be both rational and trans-rational. Emotion can play a powerful energetic role – it is persuasive and compelling, and it can be the form through which a deeper wisdom expresses itself.

However, any tool can be misused. A dialogue mapper can raise the level of decision-making transparency, or can selectively map only one subgroup's participation. He or she can help the group focus on the issues instead of the interpersonal dynamics, or can block the expression of feelings and the discussion of emotional topics. He or she can guide a group through an organizational minefield, or can hold a group hostage to an agenda. He or she can chart the lines of inter-stakeholder rivalry, or suppress the delicate and nuanced sub-channels of human communication.

The clearing provided for a group's collective intelligence to emerge is a function of the dialogue mapper's skill and intention. The collaborative display is still just a tool in the hands of a human practitioner. I have tried in this book to convey the best practices I know of for promoting ethical and humane uses of dialogue mapping. But every dialogue mapping session is a learning experience, and I am still very much a learner myself. Dialogue mappers are bound to make mistakes. What will moderate the impact of those 'learning opportunities' is the intention to serve the group and the commitment to raising their quality of dialogue and shared understanding.

Dialogue mapping can be a superb engine of effective discourse. It augments a group's collective intelligence, especially when the group is dealing with a wicked problem. However, there are situations where it may be appropriate to turn off the display, stop typing, and simply listen and be. These include:

- *Conversations about meeting process.* When a group is trying to decide when to take a break, for example, or discussing the kind of facilitation they want.
- *Interpersonal conflict.* Sometimes you can facilitate through an argument by using the dialogue map to keep the conflicting parties clear about their language and meaning and helping them be clear and explicit about what the issues are. At other times a more directive or therapeutic technique might cut through

the surface dance and facilitate a deeper conversation and reconciliation.

- *Off-the-record conversations.* If you get the feeling that someone in the group wants to speak freely without concern that their comments are being captured in writing, check in with them. Don't capture statements that might be inappropriate in the group memory. Listen carefully for the possibility that the sensitive topic, if framed appropriately, can be brought to the light of day.

- *Highly open-ended conversations.* When a new group assembles for the first time, the nature of the conversation tends to be more about relationships than content. Content is often discussed, but the dominant dynamic is social – participants are getting to know each other, building trust, establishing credentials, creating coalitions, and so on. This is not a time for vigorous mapping and validation. It may be OK to keep the display up, but it is often best just to capture questions and action items in this phase.

- *Emotional issues.* When someone is feeling very strongly about an issue, and needs to expose those feelings with a group, usually it is best to let that energy play out without trying to capture it. The typical corporate setting is excessively confining as it is, without stifling emotional experience by trying to diagram it. When feelings have cooled, it may be appropriate to map some of the content that was revealed along with the feelings.

As a dialogue mapper you must remember that the dialogue map is a sketch of the tip of a social iceberg. The vast majority of what is going on among the participants in a meeting is submerged – it is the rich and mysterious network of connections, energies, and dynamics among the members of the group. The tip of this iceberg is the rational structure of explicit verbal interactions as they are exposed to the light of day, and it floats on the much larger portion beneath the surface. The map you construct with the group reveals certain important features of this tip, and may give some clues about what is deeper, but it is always incomplete and superficial. The deep structure remains hidden in the depths, and you must judge when to focus the group on the tip (or to view the 'tip' as indicating what's in the depths), and when to let the deeper dynamics play out without collaborative display.

There is one more occasion when you might stop dialogue mapping . . . you might even turn off the display. That is when a group is in that transcendental state of grace known as *true dialogue*. If participants are totally engaged with each other in open and supportive listening, if the conversation is filled with articulate, rich, textured expressions of heart and each one builds on the one before it, if there is a mood of spiritual unity and soulful connection, and if the group has no need for a sketch of the 'tip of the iceberg' . . . why map it? Sit back and enjoy the ride!

Is Dialogue Mapping Artificial?

The question also arises, isn't dialogue mapping an artificial way of conducting meetings? Doing dialogue mapping in a meeting is more work, and it involves adding computers and display screens and an extra player to an otherwise very simple and ancient ritual.

To this concern I say, 'Yes, definitely.' Dialogue mapping is artificial. Unfortunately, the whole work environment is artificial. The pace at which technology drives the business process is artificial. The level of social complexity on large projects is artificial. The technical complexity of projects is artificial. The level of fragmentation in our society and in our organizations is artificial.[4]

As we saw in Chapter 1, the conditions surrounding most modern projects – wicked problems and social complexity – are inherently fragmenting, and behave like forces that are constantly tearing away at coherence, clarity, alignment, and momentum. Under these stressful conditions, human behavior patterns tend to reduce to the lowest common denominator. These levels of stress, and the behavior patterns evoked, are most artificial and unnatural.

As an individual you have a choice in how you deal with this fragmented and artificial environment. One is to choose a more natural environment. This is an increasingly popular choice in industries where 'burn out' is a common phenomenon. You might buy a house in a small, rural farming community, get to know your neighbors, and make your living doing whatever it is you love, working with your hands, making candles or custom furniture. Perhaps you retire and go back to school. Perhaps you buy a sailboat and head for the South Pacific. Getting out of the artificial environment is a thoroughly rational and valid choice.

Another approach is to take on the fragmentation and embrace anything that offers to create coherence for your organization or project teams. Find expedient means for dealing with intense social complexity. Create techniques, even if artificial, to help people listen to and have compassion for each other. Apply technologies that promote shared understanding and shared commitment.

Living far away from the ones you love is an artifice of the modern post-industrial era. The telephone and email are an artificial way of dealing with that distance that reduces its harmful impact. Similarly, wicked problems and the fragmentation they create are artifices of the postmodern era. Collaborative display and dialogue mapping are artificial ways of dealing with the harmful impact of fragmentation.

Does Dialogue Mapping Slow Groups Down?

Anne Lindbergh told the story of André Gide who traveled fast through the jungles of Africa. One morning the native guides sat in a circle and refused to leave the camp. When Gide urged them to get moving they looked at him and with firmness said, 'Don't hurry us – we are waiting for our souls to catch up with us.' Many of us are ahead of our souls.

Heuerman and Olson, 1998

There's a wonderful cartoon that shows a very animated meeting in which everyone is talking at once, and one person is telling his bewildered neighbor, 'If we all talk at once we can cover a lot more material in one meeting.' The 'go fast' culture of life at Internet speed demands peak performance at every moment. This need for speed is deeply ingrained in many commercial high-tech organizations.

When a group first experiences dialogue mapping it can be a jolt – mapping the conversation takes more time, and time is scarce. Meetings take too big a chunk out of the workday as it is without slowing things down to carefully listen to each other and create a representation of our interactions!

What is missed in this rush is the cost of charging through important conversations. Most of us are very familiar with the sensation that 'we've had this conversation before' during a meeting. Sometimes you have go slow to go fast. If the necessary result of a meeting is that the participants reach shared understanding about an issue and shared commitment to a path forward, hurrying through the meeting often just means you have to do it again, perhaps with more people, or fewer, or different, but for many participants it will be an unproductive and frustrating rehash.

So, if a client expresses the concern that dialogue mapping a meeting might slow the group down, I simply review the desired outcomes with him or her. What is it that we need to achieve during the session? If high levels of shared understanding (often incorrectly referred to as 'consensus') and shared commitment are needed, then it's clear that something other than the usual meeting process is required. Listening, care, and rigor are required. For each new client, on the first time out the choice to use dialogue mapping is an experiment to see if the group really can get to a high level of ownership without getting lost in the weeds. After that, clients start learning how to set up the maps and the agenda to maximize the value of dialogue mapping sessions.

Reduced Forms of Dialogue Mapping

There are actually a couple of options in between full-on dialogue mapping and just sitting and listening to the discussion. The first is to pause in the capture and simply listen with the display still on. As we saw in Chapter 5 (on the listening cycle) there are times when it is appropriate to let the conversation run on without capturing anything. Normally, at some point you will intervene and get the group to help you capture the key points of that interaction in the map.

Another way to deal with the more delicate circumstances described above would be to let the conversation run on and *not* intervene for a recapitulation. You might simply ask, 'Was there anything from that last interaction that needs to be captured in the map?' If there is any summary or action item from the uncaptured conversation, someone will point it out. In effect, you are exempting that particular interaction from being captured in the map.

Another option is to keep capturing but turn off the display. The comments are captured in IBIS, and a map gets created, but the group is not looking at it or interacting with it. Obviously, you can't get any validation this way, so errors don't get caught, the group doesn't have any ownership of the map, and you can't contribute to or upgrade the conversation. Such a 'dark display' mode might be appropriate for a setting in which the group members don't mind having a record but, for whatever reason, they simply don't want to deal with or interact with the map. (Note that this is essentially the same as the situation in which the display is on but participants simply ignore it – there's no error correction, no ownership, and no value added. This is why, when the display is on, validation of the map is key to the group having ownership of the map.)

As a way of dealing with delicate issues or group tension, dark display is probably not a good alternative. However, it can be a good way to practice IBIS mapping until you are confident enough to hook up to a projector and guide the group with your map.

In summary, an important dialogue mapping skill is pacing the group and being in rapport with the wide range of individual and collective needs that surface as they collaborate. The largest part of this pacing is the rhythm of capture and validation, but another part is knowing when to stop mapping, and when to turn the display off and find other ways to contribute to collective intelligence.

Notes

1. Compendium is a direct successor of QuestMap.
2. 'Politics' and 'political' are generally used in two distinct ways: as relating to the affairs of government or the state, and, more commonly in organizations, in a pejorative sense to refer to 'artful and often dishonest practices' or 'based on or motivated by partisan or self-serving objectives.' I am using the terms primarily in this latter, pejorative sense.
3. It can also serve as a 'Trojan horse' – i.e. even without an explicit commitment to making the change, by engaging people in dialogue mapping they can start to converse more democratically without even realizing it.
4. The reasons for this level of artificiality and fragmentation are beyond the scope of this book. Much has been written about it elsewhere. See, for example, Ken Wilber's *The Marriage of Sense and Soul*.

9
Decisions, Decisions

*D*ecide: ***1a.*** *To settle conclusively all contention or uncertainty about*: decide a case; decided the dispute in favor of the workers. ***b.*** *To make up one's mind about*: decide what to do. ***2.*** *To influence or determine the outcome of*: A few votes decided the election. ***3.*** *To cause to make or reach a decision.*

American Heritage Dictionary, 2000

Let no one say that taking action is hard. Action is aided by courage, by the moment, by impulse, and the hardest thing in the world is making a decision.

Franz Grillparzer (Libussa (1872), Act III)

Groupthink: The act or practice of reasoning or decision-making by a group, especially when characterized by uncritical acceptance or conformity to prevailing points of view.

American Heritage Dictionary, 2000

In this final chapter, we end on decision making because it is the missing piece of the collaboration puzzle. Decisions are the primary work product of meetings and the engine of project progress. Decisions are the basis for coordinated action. At the same time, decisions and decision making are surrounded by a mythology that creates hesitation, fear and suffering, especially for managers and team leaders, who are often supposed to be the Decision Makers.

Dialogue mapping offers a definite approach to decision making . . . but it may not be what you expect.

One criticism that has been leveled at dialogue mapping is that it doesn't support decision making. There is some truth in this. IBIS and dialogue mapping are very helpful in the exploratory phase of problem solving, when the group is brainstorming options and exploring tradeoffs. But at the end of the day, nothing we have discussed about dialogue mapping tells you what the right decision is. That can be a problem. I've had people tell me, 'Why did we go to all the trouble to create that whole diagram if the system can't tell us what the decision should be?' (When we were selling the QuestMap software we had an inside joke about which key controlled the 'Decide-O-Matic' command.)

This chapter is about the dialogue mapping approach to making decisions. Box 9.1 has the formula, just to break the suspense.

Box 9.1 Decision-making technique for dialogue mapping

Pick one of the Ideas, and mark it as a Decision (see Figure 9.1).

Some readers may be unsatisfied with this approach. Where is the analysis? you may ask. Where are the criteria? Where are the weights and costs and utility estimates? Where is the quantitative calculation on the return on investment? And so on.

Let's be clear: there's no such thing as an inherently right or wrong decision, especially when it comes to wicked problems. There is no 'right answer' to figure out, and there is no algorithm to figure it out

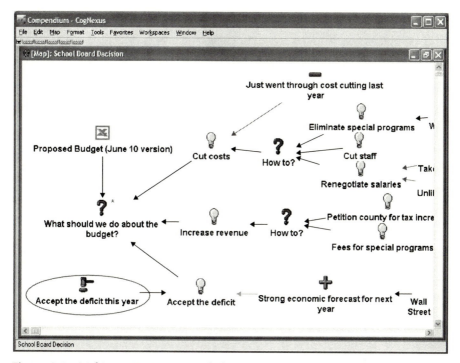

Figure 9.1 Making a Decision in a dialogue map
Note: The hammer and gavel icon in the lower left records the school board's decision.

with. Logic and data will not lead you to a good decision. The validity measure for decisions in postmodern organizations is not right/wrong or good/bad, it is about ownership. *The best decision is the one that has the broadest and deepest commitment to making it work.* To see this most clearly, consider a decision (no matter how technically correct) that no one accepts or follows – it's not really a decision, is it? Literally, what makes a decision is that people accept it as a decision. What makes it a 'good decision' is the depth and breadth of acceptance and commitment.

Some people object that this takes away any natural sense of a decision's inherent goodness or badness. That is true, and that is the point: good or bad *according to whom?* A similar objection goes like this: suppose there is broad ownership for a bad decision – does that make it a good decision? This is either a semantic salad or a deep ethical question, and goes beyond the scope of this book.

In the organizational project setting, what this means is that you don't have to worry about picking the *wrong* Idea as the decision (because there's no such thing as a wrong Idea), but you do have to avoid picking an Idea that doesn't have ownership. (In other settings a decision can be made by an authority and validated purely by force . . . legal sanctions, police, armies, etc. This doesn't weaken the need for shared understanding.)

So the question becomes, 'How to get the broadest and deepest ownership?' In part, through a process that gives the broadest and deepest participation in the decision-making process. That is, include all the stakeholders, and let the group explore the problem and solution spaces. Ownership also comes from the *story* that the group creates together, the story about what the problem is and what the constraints and drivers are and what the solution is and why that's such a good solution. For some people, ownership is enhanced by quantitative analysis, or modeling, or simulations, or focus groups, or prototypes. Logic and data are important elements of story telling in modern society. All of these elements that help build ownership emerge naturally as a group wrestles with a problem, and all of them can be included in the dialogue map. Indeed, the map *is* a story about the problem-solving process. It is also a model of the conversations that led to the decision.

One note of caution: there is a problem with the term 'ownership' (and 'buy-in') – it leaves room for an interpretation in which a few options are offered (e.g. from management), and the group's task is to own what is offered. However, in real decision making, authentic participation actually *creates* the reality in which the group is preparing to commit to the decision, whatever it turns out to be:

> Think about what happens in your experience when you want to get a plan accepted. . . . Even if the plan is excellent, it will be a long meeting in which the plan will be dissected, criticized, thrown out, brought back, and finally, almost always, approved in its initial form with only a few slight modifications. All of those participants, like the best scientists, need to observe the plan in detail, exploring its edges, searching out its interior, playing with its potentialities. (Wheatley, 1992, p. 67)

The spirit of dialogue mapping goes beyond giving participants a chance to provide their inputs on a fixed set of options. The possibility is that along with exploring the options the group also explores the nature of the problem . . . what is the *real issue* . . . what do we really care about . . . what have we been blind to?

This exploratory process results in a 'mature' dialogue map, one in which all the question types are represented, all the options described, and all the cases made. Mature maps often have many sub-maps, representing important ancillary or background conversations. (We'll review a checklist for map maturity at the end of the chapter.)

Now, I'm going to make a claim that may seem fantastic or idealistic, but it is nonetheless my experience of dialogue mapping with groups: *What makes decision making hard is lack of shared understanding. Once a group has thoroughly mapped a problem and its potential solutions, the decision itself is often obvious and natural!*

In other words, all that stuff about how hard decisions are to make, and how you need lots of data and reams of analysis and research and reports to make a good decision . . . is all a bunch of hooey. *What human beings need to make a decision is solid shared understanding about the problem and the solution space.*

What do We Need from a Decision?

A weak man has doubts before a decision; a strong man has them afterwards.

> Karl Kraus (*Beim Wort genommen* (1955), trans.
> Harry Zohn (1990) *Half-Truths and One-and-a-Half Truths*,
> University of Chicago Press)

A decision is the action an executive must take when he has information so incomplete that the answer does not suggest itself.

> Adm. Arthur W Radford (quoted in *Time*, 25 February 1957)

If the decision-making technique (choose an Idea and mark it) works, then why not just start the meeting, map out the root Question and the competing Ideas, and get the group to vote on which option they want? That should take ten, maybe 15 minutes. If it's just a matter of picking one idea, why agonize over it? (Indeed, groups frequently use this level of dialogue and exploration in making minor decisions.) This 'spin-the-dial' approach has some serious shortcomings, however:

- The selected Idea may not work (it may just *seem* like a good Idea at the time).
- There may be a much better Idea that was overlooked or not even considered.
- The selected Idea may have so little shared understanding that the implementation is hopelessly botched.

- The selected Idea may have so little ownership that the decision is abandoned as soon as an obstacle or objection arises.
- There may be stakeholders who are so alienated by lack of inclusion in the decision-making process that they actively sabotage the decision.

Lack of buy-in is an especially expensive and insidious pitfall. Some people don't worry about arguing against an idea they don't like, they just quietly resolve not to go along with it. If their participation is essential to the success of the idea, they simply don't follow through, they don't do what they said they would do. After all, everyone is busy – no one will take them to task for noncompliance. This is called a 'pocket veto' – you find out a key player disagreed with an idea because after the meeting they sabotaged it.

How do you avoid the pitfalls listed above? What kind of process creates robust and durable decisions?

Participation. Inclusion. The more authentic the participation, the higher the collective intelligence, and the more likely it is that the selected Idea will work, will be the best among the options, will have good shared understanding and strong shared commitment.[1] Dialogue mapping is simply a way of augmenting the group's collective intelligence, making the dialogue process more creative and effective.

Two Theories on When to Decide

Exhaustion and exasperation are frequently the handmaidens of legislative decision.

> *Barber B Conable Jr* (quoted in *Time*, 22 October 1984)

At the constitutional level where we work, 90 percent of any deci-sion is emotional. The rational part of us supplies the reasons for supporting our predilections.

> William O Douglas (to Justice Potter Stewart on why
> Vietnam War veterans were arrested for peaceful
> protest on steps of the Supreme Court building)

As a dialogue mapper, you should know when it's time to exercise the decision-making technique (remember: choose one Idea and mark it). There are two competing theories about how you know when it's time to make the decision, the *learning through deciding* theory and the *when it's ripe* theory.

The *learning through deciding* theory says, don't worry too much about finding the right time to make a decision – get the group to go through several decision-making cycles, and use the cycles to raise the energy and increase learning. It's a very organic, postmodern approach to the nerve-racking process of making a decision, and it's hard to pull off in some organizational cultures, but it is based on empirical evidence about how decision processes really work (Garvin and Roberto, 2001).

The traditional view is that there are two phases of collective work: divergence and convergence. Divergence brings out issues, ideas, information – it may well seem like the group members are diverg-ing from each other. Convergence is about eliminating options, zeroing in on arguments and key criteria, and finally making one or several decisions. You can see these phases when dialogue mapping is in use, but you also can see a less linear possibility. As the overall map grows from a single Question to a large set of interlocking sub-maps, the potentiality of closure is there at any moment. Map matu-rity is relative. More importantly, dialogue mapping is based on the cognitive reality of *opportunity-driven problem solving* (see Chapter 1), so decisions are seen as opportunities for accelerated learning, not as the end point of the process. Sometimes you have to stand on the other side of the decision for a moment to really appreciate its consequences.

I was working with a group of technologists from the Air National Guard several years ago. The topic was to design a scheme for evaluating technology suggestions from across the whole organization. We had gone through the background part of the meeting, and we had mapped out why this was a problem now, what the schedule was for resolving it, and some other constraints. We had mapped out the basic requirements for the new system. We had the main question in the map, 'How should we implement the suggestion processing system?,' and there were a few ideas about parts of it, but it felt half-hearted and vague. There was a pause. I said, 'Does anybody happen to have an idea about an overall solution?' After a moment a lieutenant sitting on my left said, 'Well, I have given this a little thought, and I do have one idea about how this might work.' So I got him to elaborate on his idea and I mapped it out. After another half an hour of tweaking and elaboration that idea was adopted by the group for implementation. They made a decision. Until the lieutenant spoke the mood of the group was a cautious, linear, analytical discussion – it was quite proper and good form as design discussions go. It just didn't have any energy. Getting a proposal on the table galvanized the group's collective intelligence and turned a long tedious design session into an engaged and thoughtful race to the finish.

Since, as a dialogue mapper, you know that the purpose of making a decision is to stimulate learning and thinking, you can call for a decision at any point. And as the dialogue unfolds and the map grows and matures, more and more shared understanding and shared commitment infuses the group. The motto of *learning through deciding* is 'Decide early, decide often!'

The *when it's ripe* theory is more traditional, and is less likely to scare your client. In this approach, you make a careful and orchestrated move into the moment of decision. You might even have some kind of ceremony, as I did in one meeting where one participant made a big show of putting a large checkmark next to the selected option as we went through a series of decisions. For this approach, you have to know when the group has enough shared understanding and shared commitment and is ready to decide.

In my experience, there are two keys to knowing that a group is ready to decide:

1   You can feel it, energetically . . . there's a kind of settling, a sense of clarity, a readiness to commit. Or . . .
2   You're out of time.

Obviously the first condition, often referred to as 'consensus,' is preferable to the second. But in practice, there is a limited amount of time available for the process of solving a problem and making implementation decisions, and groups have to settle for getting the *most* ownership and understanding possible in the allocated time.

Both the *learning through deciding* and *when it's ripe* approaches work. The main difference between them is that the latter is more orderly and linear and plays inside the paradigm that there is this One Right Decision, while the former is more energetic, promotes faster learning, and can result in big time savings. Because it is less traditional the former approach takes some getting used to, both for you and the group. We'll explore both approaches in more depth later.

An Example: Substation Workstation Decision

According to the decision-making rule, all that's needed to make a decision is selecting one of the ideas as the decision. What if there are two sides and there is no way that either side is going to submit to the other? In that case you'll have to appeal the decision to a higher authority . . . kick it upstairs.[2]

This happened with an electric utility company client of mine. The issue was, 'Which workstation should be the standard for use in the substations?' There was the proprietary system camp and the UNIX workstation camp. These two groups had been at war for months . . . some said years. A colleague and I were called in to dialogue map the meeting where these two groups were to present their cases and the decision was to be made. First, the proprietary system group made their case. They had presentations by their best people, and as they talked we built a map of the whole case for the proprietary system. Then the UNIX group made their presentations – they even brought in an outside expert who testified that UNIX was the only way to go. We mapped out that case as well.

By lunch what we had created was a very large map that made it clear there was no 'right' answer. The proprietary systems were more efficient, the programs already existed, and the field personnel were already trained in using these systems. The UNIX system would require some reprogramming and retraining, but would allow the sub-stations to be maintained and upgraded and integrated with other parts of the electricity transmission system more easily.[3]

It was clear: This was not going to be a consensus decision. It had the feeling of a 'religious' issue – for each side it was black and white. We couldn't just take a vote . . . how would we decide who got to vote? So we asked the group, 'Suppose we settle this by getting a decision from higher up. Who would you trust to make this decision for you? Who, if we got them in here, would be able to make the best decision, and no matter what they decided, you would accept and implement their decision?' After a few minutes of discussion the group agreed on three executives whose judgement, if those three agreed on either option, the group would trust as the best decision.

As it happened, we were able to get all three executives to drop in after lunch. They listened intently as the groups presented their respective pieces of the dialogue map. All the information was there, all the arguments explicit. After hearing both sides they called a break, stepped outside for a few minutes, and then came back in and announced their decision. They said it wasn't an easy decision for them, but that, from where they sat, the UNIX option was techni-cally stronger and offered a better fit with the company's strategic direction. They said it was clear that a lot of hard work had gone into thinking out the pros and cons of the two options, and that the map had really helped them see and balance the key issues involved. They asked both sides to set aside all their past differences and work together to implement the UNIX option as quickly as possible.

This is an example of the *when it's ripe* approach. In the end, the dialogue map served to help the opposing sides marshal their best arguments and make them clearly and succinctly, and it served the decision makers in quickly absorbing all of the facts and points of view about the issues and making their decision. Moreover, the 'losing' proprietary system group knew that they had been heard and that the decision was fair.

Checklist for Decision Making

Our passional nature not only lawfully may, but must, decide an option between propositions, whenever it is a genuine option that cannot by its nature be decided on intellectual grounds; for to say, under such circumstances, 'Do not decide, but leave the question open,' is itself a passional decision – just like deciding yes or no – and is attended with the same risk of losing the truth.

William James (*New World* (1896) in Alburey Casteu (ed.) (1948) *Essays in Pragmatism*, New York: Hafner)

To recap, we have described the decision-making process as a matter of selecting one Idea (or several Ideas) in a dialogue map and marking them as the decision. We claimed that the single most important thing to be paying attention to is the ownership of this emerging decision, and that the process of building broad ownership requires genuine engagement and participation from the full range of stakeholders. And we claimed that more mature maps indicate higher levels of understanding and commitment among the members of a group.

In this section we review key elements of the preceding chapters and offer specific techniques to drive toward closure and bring a group to a decision using dialogue mapping. The steps offered here are not meant to be followed as a linear formula; rather, they are a sort of checklist that will help you and the group work the dialogue map to sufficient maturity that it is ready for a robust decision to be taken. These steps are:

1 Ask all the key Questions.
2 Case making for key Ideas.
3 Case making against key Ideas.
4 Endorsements.
5 Validation of criteria.
6 Making the Decision.

The key to using this checklist effectively is to always pay attention to the levels of ownership among the stakeholders.

Ask All the Key Questions

You will have at least one deontic ('What should we do?') or instrumental ('How should we do X?') Question in the map. There may be a whole set of decisions to be made, but there is often one Big Question that, when decided, will feel like crossing over a mountain range. Before resolving the Big Question it was mostly uphill, after it is mostly downhill. Other decisions and dependencies will become clear once the Big Question is resolved. (We call this the 'Big Question' because, although it may have been the root Question at some point, it may no longer be the root Question. More abstract, but less critical, Questions may have been placed to the left of it through 'left-hand' moves (see Chapter 7).)

The Big Question will have a criterial Question ('What are the criteria?') linked to it, and there will be a few criterial Ideas on it. There is likely to be a stakeholder Question, either 'Who are the stakeholders?' or 'Who should the stakeholders be?' . . . or both. Since the map is fairly mature the other Question types will also be represented. There are likely to be a few meaning Questions, and a few factual Questions. (If all of this seems mysterious, it's time to review Chapter 6.)

Case Making for Key Ideas

Since the decision will be a selected Idea, it's important that you and the group feel confident that all of the Ideas that are contenders for the resolution of the Big Question have been captured. Although you can often feel when the group has Ideas in the map that reflect a bit of 'out-of-the-box' thinking, it is usually good to probe for any more outlying potential solutions that might be lurking out there. You ask (pointing to the Big Question), 'I just want to check now . . . are there any other viable ways to resolve our question here?' (Remember, whenever you interact with the group you are pointing at a specific element in the map and shifting your gaze between that element and the group members. As you speak you make frequent references to the map with 'here,' 'this Question,' 'these Ideas,' 'that one,' etc. See Chapters 2 and 5.) A moment of silence can be a good thing at this point.

Unless I am running a brainstorming process, I always like to get at least one Pro (one supporting argument) from the person who offers an Idea. Usually they include this with their idea: 'What if we shifted the inventory database to Server B? That would lighten the peak loads on Server A and give us a better load balance.' (That's an Idea and two Pros.) If they don't include the support, I ask for it, something like, 'And what shall I put as a reason for doing that?'

The fact that some arguments are stronger than others makes it tempting to add some kind of 'strength' rating to the IBIS notation, e.g. high-medium-low or a 5-point scale. The problem with such systems is that as soon as you try to codify argument strength you have to recognize that it is a relative and subjective judgement. An argument that is 'high' strength for one person might seem quite weak to another; what strength code would you use? There may be specific settings in which it is helpful, but in general dialogue mapping seems to work better if argument strength is left implicit.

It is quite possible to have a situation where all Ideas listed have significant objections (Cons). This indicates that the map is not as mature as it should be for a decision. It's almost impossible to select an Idea as the decision if it has a significant unresolved objection. Good design practice stipulates that the group should pick the best elements of the best Ideas and creatively blend them together into a new Idea or Ideas that get around the worst of these objections. I've had at least one occasion when it was clear that none of the proposed Ideas would fly and that a decision was not going to be possible. Then, seemingly out of the blue, one of the participants said, 'Well, now, I don't know if this will work, but what if we . . . ,' and described a new synthetic proposal that did not have the onerous objections possessed by the other Ideas. I captured the Idea and the arguments for it. After working on it for a few minutes the group selected that Idea as their decision.

Another situation that can happen is that there are no big objections to any of the proposed Ideas, but neither is anyone very excited about them. This could be an important warning sign: you may not have the right people assembled, or you may not have the best Big Question in the map yet. Other times it can simply be that the group just hasn't come up with a good enough proposal yet, but with a bit of encouragement they'll engage and come up with something they can rally around. Remember my Air National Guard group? The pivotal stimulus was asking, 'Does anybody happen to have an Idea about an overall solution?'[4] If you do flush out any new Ideas, have the group make a case for them as you put them in the map.

Of course, it is always possible that the problem is wicked enough that none of the existing Ideas will fly with the group, and nobody has any better proposals up their sleeve. Perhaps this means it's time to end the meeting and send everyone off to do more research and networking. Or it may be that, precisely by continuing through these steps and driving the group toward a decision, you can flush out new ideas, hidden agendas, or fresh energy.

Case Making Against Key Ideas

The point in this step is to make sure that important arguments that might be lurking around, especially 'killer arguments,' have been stated and captured in the map. As important as they are for sound decision making, objecting arguments can be hard to tease out. (Indeed, reluctance to think critically is what fuels 'groupthink.')

In some cultures it is impolite to openly object to someone else's idea. In my experience this is more true in situations where the subject matter is abstract or political, or both. Engineering groups are refreshing in this respect – if someone sees a technical problem with an idea they'll come right out and say it. Dialogue mapping is a snap in these situations, because the IBIS Pros and Cons concisely capture two common conversational moves in the design process.

In more politicized situations, if someone has an objection to a proposal (let's say they think it will be too expensive to implement) they may do one of the following:

- State their objection as a question . . . 'Would that be over our budget?' (Or even, 'Have you run this idea past the folks in finance?').
- Formulate their objection as a Pro for another Idea . . . 'Bob's proposal X is clearly in our budget.'
- Try to change the subject.
- Wait and hope that someone else will say it.

In these situations, I have found that it is best to play along. (There was a time when I might 'help' a group communicate more directly by capturing diplomatic moves as what I was sure they were: objections. It just didn't go over that well. As powerful as a big, honest, minus sign is in the map, it rubs some people the wrong way. With experience I learned that it was better to map in the local dialect.) If someone states an objection as a Question, go ahead and capture it as a Question. Sure, it doesn't have the clarity in the map that a Con would have, but the group understands what it means, and that really is the main thing. And, with further discussion, they may revise it into a Con.

An alternative to putting objections in the map as Cons is to instead use a Question such as 'What are the disadvantages?' linked to the Idea. The objections are then Ideas on this Question, instead of Cons on the Idea, which softens their visual impact a bit. (This structure makes a mess of the map from an IBIS standpoint, but sometimes this is the only way to get critical thinking accepted in the map.)

As decision time approaches (and as local customs permit) you may ask, 'Are there any objections that we haven't captured to these main ideas?' Sometimes this will flush out a 'killer argument,' a Con so compelling that it kills the Idea on the spot. Of course, you will capture the Con (emphasis, exclamation points, and underlines are allowed in the map, but unnecessary), and you may also find that everyone is fine with *'retiring'* the Idea itself.

Notationally, retiring an Idea is simply putting it in parentheses . . . '(<Bad idea>).' Retiring an Idea is a powerful convergence step. After all, making a decision is, operationally, equivalent to retiring all the nonselected Ideas. If you can retire a few Ideas along the way, it narrows the field of strong, viable Ideas for the group to consider. Note: Retiring an Idea is a consensus operation – if there is even one person who thinks it should be left in play, don't retire it. Also, instead of putting a retired Idea in parentheses, it is tempting to delete the Idea (and any Pros and Cons and sub-Questions hanging from it) from the map, but this is rarely a good idea because it weakens the group memory.

As a final check on the case making against key Ideas, ask the group to consider the map from the standpoint of stakeholders who aren't present. Refer to the stakeholder question and ask, 'If you consider this map from the standpoint of these stakeholders, are there any other Pros or Cons that they would come up with?'

Endorsements

Getting endorsements for Ideas is a fast and fun way to move the group toward closure. Endorsements are like voting, but you are not making the decision, you're just finding out where the group stands on the options so far. You may have to emphasize this: 'We are not making a decision right now. We just want to find out where the energy is in the room.' Here are the steps to endorsements:

1 Starting with the top Idea on the Big Question, ask the group, 'Does anyone want to endorse this idea?' A few people might raise their hands. Count the hands.

2 Make a Pro to the Idea with the label 'Endorsed' and the number of endorsers. (If the group is small enough, you might record their initials instead; this feels more personal and helps the group keep track of who is endorsing what.)

3 Repeat this process on each Idea, so that every Idea on the Big Question has, for example, 'Endorsed: 3' on it. To show that this isn't voting, I usually allow participants to endorse as many Ideas as they want to.

4 One thing that will stand out now: any Ideas with zero endorsements. If there are no endorsements for an Idea, ask if any of the absent stakeholders would endorse it. If still no endorsements, suggest that the Idea be retired. Sometimes, just as you're putting the parentheses around the Idea, someone will speak up, 'OK, I'll endorse that one. It's too important to let it go yet.' (This process builds a lot of ownership in the map – people see that what gets captured – and *only* what gets captured – receives careful attention and consideration from the group.)

5 Another thing that may stand out at this point: someone who didn't endorse any Ideas. I would ask this person, 'So, there aren't any Ideas that you want to endorse?' Usually this will bring out more case making: a new Idea that's not in the map, or a new objection to a popular Idea in the map.

With any luck, a round of endorsements will retire a few Ideas, bring out some new arguments, and focus the group on the few Ideas that, because they got the most endorsements, have the most energy and likelihood of becoming the decision. It also shows the group where it is in the decision-making process. If there is one Idea that got most of the endorsements, it's clear that a consensus is emerging. If there are three Ideas that each got the same number of endorsements, there is still a lot of work to do.

Validation of Criteria

Recall the 'criterial leap' from Chapter 6? In a mature map there should be a strong correspondence between the Pros and Cons on the key Ideas and the Ideas on the criterial Question. Part of bringing the group to closure is checking this correspondence – it's a sort of map hygiene.

Have them look at the list of criteria for the Big Question. Is the list complete? Help them by picking a Con, for example, and asking, 'Is the criterion behind this argument in the list?' Capture any new criteria that get revealed in this process.

Similarly, focus the group on the top few Ideas (i.e. the ones with the most endorsements), and have them look at the criteria and see if there are any additional arguments that haven't been made. For example, there might be a criterion, 'Do as much as possible in-house.' When they consider the top Idea, someone says, 'If that was our decision we'd have to outsource the whole training process.' This is probably a new Con to the Idea.

Making the Decision

Horst Rittel, the main inventor of IBIS, used to say that there was no point having a technique for making decisions because the decision-making process was highly dependent on context: the organizational culture, history, and practices, the nature of the problem, the personalities and power relationships among the stakeholders, etc. We agree. That's why most of this chapter is not about decision making; it's about map maturity. If the map is mature, the conditions will be set for the greatest possible shared under-standing and commitment when the decision gets made . . . however that happens.

There are a few standard methods for decision making, and you are probably quite familiar with them. Here's a short list for review:

- *Authoritarian/hierarchical* – the decision is made by the person at the top of the pyramid.
- *Delegation* – the group picks one person, among equals, and empowers him or her to make the decision.
- *Majority rule* – the group votes among the options and the deci-sion goes to the one with the most votes.
- *Mediation* – two parties agree to bring in a third party to help them reach a mutually agreeable decision.

There are others and there are variations among these. The point is that there are a variety of methods to pick from. Moreover, different methods convey different levels of ownership. For example, a group will generally have more ownership of a decision that is made by majority rule than by an authority (but not always).

You may be wondering why consensus – the wonderbread of our team-based world – isn't in the list of decision methods. The reason is simple: consensus is a state, not a method. Consensus is a condi-tion in which most or all of the participants agree to the decision or judgement. True consensus takes real work, in which the participants engage in authentic dialogue, and refuse to move ahead if any par-ticipant has a strong objection. Thus the method is dialogue, followed by a 'vote', if you will, which is only a decision if no one has strong objections. The term 'consensus' is widely misused these days, as in,

'OK, we've got to move on . . . I think we have consensus to move ahead with the building project,' or 'OK, we've only a got few minutes. Let's get consensus about this decision.' In any case, dialogue mapping is an effective way to build toward consensus, whether or not the situation affords the time and energy necessary to build true consensus.

When a group is working on a problem or project, the decision-making method that will be used is usually implicit and understood by the participants. For example, in a command-and-control organization, everyone understands that, at the end of the day, the manager or the project leader is the one who actually has the authority to make the decision. Nonetheless, it is powerful to be clear and explicit with a group, especially when working on a wicked problem, about how decisions will be made. That way, everyone is working within a process in which the endgame is clear.

When the time comes, decide the question following the method. Record the decision in the map, marking the respective Idea or Ideas as the decision. That's it.

Well . . . almost. Next there will be a set of action items to capture which begin implementation of the decision.

If you are using the *learning through deciding* approach, you can use the decision method several times, each time resulting in a certain level of closure, and each time driving up new issues or options. Or you can use endorsements as a lightweight simulated decision process. Each time, the map gets more mature, and shared understanding and shared commitment grow. Even if you use the *when it's ripe* approach, it's always possible that the 'final decision' isn't final . . . that it comes back to the group for further work. This can happen, for example, when the decision failed to be ratified by a higher authority. This is when it is a blessing to have the dialogue maps of the process. You just take up where you left off . . . adding the reason the decision was rejected as a new argument in the map.

I want to close by restating the dialogue mapping approach to decision making: *What makes decision making hard is lack of shared understanding. Once a group has thoroughly mapped a problem and its potential solutions, the decision itself is often obvious and natural!*

Notes

1. See also Kim and Mauborgne, 1997 for another version of this approach.
2. This includes referring the decision to an arbitration or negotiation process.
3. Many wicked issues have this 'right versus right' quality. For a full discussion of such issues in an ethical context, see Kidder, 1996.
4 The shift here is from answering the specific question to solving the whole problem. Sometimes someone has a 'plan' that addresses the whole problem, but you don't have the right Question in the map yet, and that person is waiting for the opportunity to present his/her plan.

Appendix

Further Resources

Compendium

The main resource you will need to further explore dialogue mapping is the Compendium software, download available from the Compendium Institute at http://compendiuminstitute.org. At the time of writing Compendium is available at no cost.

The screenshots in this book were created using the 'QuestMap' skin – see 'Format', 'Icon Sets' on the menu.

The Compendium source code is also available in Open Source for those with the skills and energy to contribute to the Compendium community with improvements and extensions to the software.

Training

This book borrows heavily from the curriculum of the *Dialog Mapping Workshop*, a two-day workshop for interactive learning and practice with the basic and some advanced skills of dialogue mapping. The workshop is offered by CogNexus Institute; see http://cognexus.org.

The training materials for Compendium are being expanded and refined – see the training section of the Compendium Institute website, http://compendiuminstitute.org.

Further Reading

The CogNexus Institute website also features related articles for further reading and links to other resources: http://cognexus.org. In particular, see the Compendium section for tips and techniques on IBIS, map management, creating reports ('meeting minutes'), and other practical topics on using the software.

References

American Heritage® Dictionary of the English Language, 4th edn (2000) Boston, MA: Houghton Mifflin.

Argyris, C. and Schön, D. (1996) *Organizational Learning II: Theory, Method and Practice*, Reading, MA: Addison Wesley.

Bowker, G. C. and Star, S. L. (1999) *Sorting Things Out: Classification and Its Consequences*, Cambridge, MA: MIT Press.

Buckingham Shum, S. and Hammond, N. (1994) 'Argumentation-based design rationale: what use at what cost?', *International Journal of Human–Computer Studies*, Vol. 40, No. 4, 603–652.

Conklin, J. (2003) 'Dialog mapping: reflections on an industrial strength case study' in Kirschner, P., Buckingham Shum, S. and Carr, C. (eds) *Visualizing Argumentation: Software Tools for Collaborative and Educational Sense-Making*, London: Springer.

Conklin, J., Selvin, A., Buckingham Shum, S., and Sierhuis, M. (2003) 'Facilitated hypertext for collective sensemaking: 15 years on from gIBIS' in Weigand, H., Goldkuhl, G., and de Moor, A. (eds) *Proceedings LAP2003: Proceedings LAP'03: 8th International Working Conference on the Language-Action Perspective on Communication Modelling*, Tilburg, The Netherlands.

Cooperrider, D. L. and Whitney, W. (1999) *Appreciative Inquiry: Collaborating for Change*, San Francisco: Berrett-Koehler.

DeKoven, B. (1990) *Connected Executives: A Strategic Communications Plan*, Palo Alto, CA: Institute for Better Meetings.

Dervin, B. (1998) 'Sense making theory and practice: an overview of user interests in knowledge seeking and use', *Journal of Knowledge Management*, Vol. 2, No. 2, 36–46.

Eden, C. and Ackerman, F. (1998) *Making Strategy: The Journey of Strategic Management*, London: Sage.

Engelbart, D. C. (1963) 'A conceptual framework for the augmentation of man's intellect' in Howerton, P. W. and Weeks, D. C. (eds) *Vistas in Information Handling*, Washington, DC: Spartan Books, pp. 1–29. Also in Greif, I. (ed.) (1988) *Computer Supported Cooperative Work: A Book of Readings*, San Mateo, CA: Morgan Kaufmann Publishers, Inc., pp. 35–65.

Garvin, D. A. and Roberto, M. A. (2001) 'What you don't know about making decisions', *Harvard Business Review*, September 2001.

Guindon, R. (1990) 'Designing the design process: exploiting opportunistic thoughts', *Human–Computer Interaction*, Vol. 5, 305–344.

Heuerman, T. and Olson, D. (1998) 'Organizational mindfulness', *Self-help Magazine*, http://www.selfhelpmagazine.com/articles/wf/orgmind. html (accessed 31 March 2005).

Kidder, R. M. (1996) *How Good People Make Tough Choices: Resolving the Dilemmas of Ethical Living*, New York: Simon and Schuster.

Kim, W. C. and Mauborgne, R. (1997) 'Fair process: managing in the knowledge economy', *Harvard Business Review*, July 1997.

Kirschner, P., Buckingham Shum, S., and Carr, C. (eds) (2003) *Visualizing Argumentation: Software Tools for Collaborative and Educational Sense-Making*, London: Springer.

Kunz, W. and Rittel, H. (1970) 'Issues as elements of information systems', Working Paper 131, Berkeley, CA: The Institute of Urban and Regional Development, University of California, Tel: (510) 642-4874, email: iurd@uclink.berkeley.edu.

Moran, T. and Carroll, J. (eds) (1996) *Design Rationale: Concepts, Techniques, and Use*, Mahwah, NJ: Lawrence Erlbaum Associates.

Palus, C. J. and Drath, W. H. (2001) 'Putting something in the middle: an approach to dialogue', *Reflections*, Vol. 3, No. 2, 28–39.

Pascal, R., Millemann, M., and Gioia, L. (2000) *Surfing the Edge of Chaos*, New York: Three Rivers Press.

Rischard, J. F. (2002) *High Noon: Twenty Global Issues, Twenty Years to Solve Them*, New York: Basic Books.

Rittel, H. (1972a) 'On the planning crisis: systems analysis of the "first and second generations"', Reprint. No. 107, Berkeley, CA: Institute of Urban and Regional Development, University of California.

Rittel, H. (1972b) 'Structure and usefulness of planning information systems', *Bedrifts Økonomen*, No. 8, Norway. Also Reprint No. 108, Berkeley, CA: The Institute of Urban and Regional Development, University of California.

Rittel, H. and Noble, D. (1989) 'Issue-based information systems for design', Working Paper 492, Berkeley, CA: The Institute of Urban and Regional Development, University of California.

Rittel, H. and Webber, M. (1973) 'Dilemmas in a general theory of planning', *Policy Sciences*, Vol. 4, 155–169. Also available as Reprint No. 86, Berkeley, CA: Institute of Urban and Regional Development, University of California.

Rosenhead, J. V. and Mingers, J. (2001) *Rational Analysis in a Problematic World Revisited*, Chichester: John Wiley and Sons, Ltd.

Rough, J. (1991) 'Choice-creating: how to solve impossible problems', *The Journal of Quality and Participation*, September.

Rough, J. (1997) 'Dynamic facilitation and the magic of self-organizing change', *The Journal of Quality and Participation*, June.

Saaty, T. L. (1999) *Decision Making for Leaders: The Analytic Hierarchy Process for Decisions in a Complex World*, Pittsburg, PA: RWS Publications.

Schrage, M. (1995) *No More Teams: Mastering the Dynamics of Creative Collaboration*, New York: Currency Doubleday.

Schwartz, P. (1996) *The Art of the Long View*, New York: Doubleday.

Selvin, A. and Sierhuis, M. (1999) 'Argumentation in different CSCA project types' in *Workshop on Computer-Supported Collaborative Argumentation, Conference on Computer-Supported Collaborative Learning*, Stanford, CA (12–15 December 1999) (http://d3e.open.ac.uk/cscl99/Selvin-RelArg/Selvin-RelArg-paper.html).

Simon, Herbert A. (1969) *The Sciences of the Artificial*, 2nd edn, Cambridge, MA: MIT Press.

van der Heijden, K. (1996) *Scenarios: The Art of Strategic Conversation*, Chichester: John Wiley & Sons, Ltd.

Weick, Karl E. (1995) *Sensemaking in Organizations*, London: Sage.

Weisbord, M. and Janoff, S. (2000) Future Search – An Action Guide to Finding Common Ground in Organizations & Communities, San Francisco: Berrett-Koehler.

Wheatley, M. J. (1992) *Leadership and the New Science: Learning about Organization from an Orderly Universe*, San Francisco: Berrett-Koehler.

Wilbur, K. (1996) *A Brief History of Everything*, Boston, MA: Shambhala.

Wilbur, K. (1998) *The Marriage of Sense and Soul: Integrating Science and Religion*, New York: Random House.

Index

Note: The abbreviation 'IBIS' stands for 'issue-based information system'.